THE EFFECTIVE

SCHOOL DEPARTMENT HEAD

THE EFFECTIVE

SCHOOL DEPARTMENT HEAD

Michael G. Callahan

PARKER PUBLISHING COMPANY, INC.

WEST NYACK, NEW YORK

To my wife Olga,
who heads the most challenging department of all;
and to my daughters Karen and Kristen,
who staff that department.

THE SCOPE AND PURPOSE OF THIS BOOK

THE EFFECTIVE SCHOOL DEPARTMENT HEAD is written for many readers.

The book is addressed to school *principals* and their administrative assistants. It offers them a practical, step-by-step guide for evaluating and improving the work of their subject area department heads or department chairmen.

It is also addressed to school *superintendents* and their administrative assistants. It provides them with an overview of the department head position as it is found in both traditional and innovative school districts. And it offers specific recommendations designed to improve that position in the schools of today—and tomorrow.

The book is also written for present and future *department heads* themselves. It provides them with a detailed model of how an effective school department head meets his many responsibilities in the areas of staff utilization, supervision, curriculum development, and departmental management.

And it is also addressed to *teachers* and *teachers of teachers* in schools of education. It offers them the first comprehensive survey of a critically important "Middle management" position which is found in most modern secondary schools.

The department head (or department chairman, as he may be titled) is found in thousands of schools throughout the United States and Canada. Each of these schools will typically have ten or twelve such teacher-leaders on its staff. Each of them supervises a group of teachers, numbering from as few as three to as many as fifty, all working in a particular subject field or other specialized area.

So great are the power and influence which these department heads traditionally exercise that to a very real degree they determine how good those schools will be.

This is true because the department head is, to begin with, the vital link between those who plan school policy and those who carry it out. If the chairman works effectively, there will be a continuous flow of essential information between administrators and teachers. In such cases, school programs of all kinds may be carried forward successfully. But if the department head does not work effectively, there will be inevitable confusion, misinformation, and misdirection. This can result in unnecessary divisions between administrative and faculty groups in a school.

Moreover, the department head plays a key part in virtually every phase of a school's operation. His influence is felt when teachers are employed and then when they are evaluated for promotion or dismissal. Under the chairman's direction, a department will construct and revise its instructional programs, purchase the materials needed to implement them, and then present them to the school and community. If the department head works effectively, then his department will be alert, dynamic, and innovative. His teachers will offer the best possible instructional programs, winning thereby valuable public support for the school and district. But if the department head does not work effectively, he may so stifle creativity and initiative within his department that teachers, students, and the community as well will all suffer as a consequence.

Administrators on all levels, department heads and teachers must be concerned about the role and functions of the school department head because, quite simply, the department leadership is big business.

The tens of thousands of department head positions established in schools throughout the country require the annual expenditure of millions of dollars for released time and salary increments. Moreover, these chairmen spend—or misspend—additional millions of dollars each year for books, instructional supplies, equipment, and similar items used in their departments. It is essential, therefore, that every district look carefully at the policies and practices which have been set up to guide the work of these department chairmen. Only in this way can school personnel on all levels be sure that their chairmen are providing quality leadership in return for the heavy demands which they make on district budgets.

This book is designed to help educators on every level conduct just such a thorough appraisal of the department head position. From this can come improvements in the performance of the chairmen themselves. And from that can come improvements in the quality of teaching which is carried on in all the classrooms of their departments.

The Effective School Department Head grew out of a year-long study of the department head position which the author conducted while on special assignment for the San Mateo Union High School District in California. As part of this project, the author studies the department headship and departmental operations as they have been discussed in the professional literature of the past decade. This research was carried out in five major libraries, including those of Stanford University and the University of California.

Following this research, the author visited nearly a score of school districts in California and Oregon, to observe both traditional and innovative approaches to providing departmental leadership in secondary schools. These visits included conferences with hundreds of administrators, department heads, and classroom teachers, to learn how they perceived the role and functions of the truly effective school department head.

This book is the result of that year of research, visitations, and conferences. It is offered with the sincere wish that it prove useful to all educators who share the author's concern for improving both the work and the position of the school department head.

Michael G. Callahan

CONTENTS

Appendix B

Appendix C

THE EFFECTIVE
SCHOOL DEPARTMENT HEAD

Part One

IMPROVING THE PERFORMANCE OF THE DEPARTMENT HEAD IN A SCHOOL

1

Understanding the Department Head's Role and Functions

Two young teachers, recently graduated from the state university, had just signed their first contracts with a large, suburban high school district.

The district's administrators were highly pleased with these newest additions to their faculty. Both had come to the district with impressive academic records, excellent personal references, and obvious determination to become good teachers. They had been carefully screened from among scores of applicants by the district's personnel officers and had been interviewed at length by the principals of the schools to which they would be assigned.

The two new instructors were equally enthusiastic about their appointments. The district, embracing half a dozen affluent, upper middle class communities, was noted for its strong, innovative leadership, its excellent salary schedules, and its support of small classes, well-stocked libraries and laboratories, and all the other essentials of a desirable teaching situation.

Six months later, one of the two beginners was successfully launched into his new career. His classes were progressing smoothly, his morale was high, and he was looking forward to a long and rewarding career as a teacher. The other new teacher, however, was so discouraged and embittered that he was seriously considering resigning from his position and leaving the teaching profession even before the end of the academic year.

What had made the difference in the experiences of the two teachers? The cause had nothing to do with community pressures, militant students, or any of the other factors which are usually cited as the underlying sources of teacher dissatisfaction. Nothing which the district superintendent or his staff had said or done had made the difference. Neither had the principals or the other administrators of the two schools involved played major roles in determining the experiences and attitudes of the two new instructors.

The real reason for the one teacher's success and the other's shattered career lay in the very different experiences which they had had with the most influential of their teaching colleagues: the heads of their departments. Unfortunately, only one chairman had worked effectively to help his new teacher adjust to the school and to the requirements of his classes.

The other chairman had adopted a casual "sink or swim" attitude toward the newcomer in his department. He had assigned the new man to teach a program which was heavily weighted with remedial classes, reserving less demanding courses for the veteran teachers with tenure in the department. Furthermore, the chairman had varied his general policy of indifference to the young teacher's needs only when he found an opportunity to point out the man's errors and inadequacies. This, the department head maintained, was the proper way to provide really effective in-service training, for it required the young teacher to correct his own shortcomings entirely by his own efforts.

Is this an exaggerated portrait? Unfortunately, as the author discovered through his research and visitations, the truth is that such experiences as those just described are far more realistic and representative than many administrators might care to admit.

The department head, for better or worse, is to be found in the majority of high schools in the United States. There he occupies a vaguely defined and constantly changing position. He is in part a classroom teacher, in part a curriculum consultant, and also in part an administrative assistant to the principal of his school. He is thus a colleague, an adviser, and a director of the teachers in his subject area.

Under effective supervision, a conscientious department head becomes an invaluable resource in the work of teacher development conducted by the district's personnel officers and the school's principal. On the other hand, without appropriate direction, a department head may become lazy, indifferent, or tyrannical, thus damaging all of the programs begun by his administrative superiors in the areas of curriculum and personnel. Such a chairman can ignore his teachers' need for help and encouragement, stifling their creativity and enthusiasm. He may even harass them to the point where, as in the example just described, good instructors eventually are driven out of the profession.

In light of the critically influential position occupied by department heads, school administrators on all levels must be alert to the need for careful, systematic, and regular reappraisal of the policies and practices established to guide chairmen in their districts. Only in this way can superintendents, directors of instruction and personnel, and principals be certain that every chairman in every school is doing what he should—as well as he can.

Such an appraisal ought to begin with a definition of the role and function of the department head in a modern school.

BRIDGING AN ADMINISTRATIVE GAP

The department head position appears in the organizational charts and faculty rosters of school districts in every state. The reason for this is simple: the chairman fills an administrative vacuum created by the rapid growth of public education in America during this century.

As school systems grow in size, enrolling larger and larger percentages of a population which is itself expanding at nearly an explosive rate, school administrators on all levels have found their problems growing in number and complexity. By necessity, superintendents and their staffs have become absorbed in the demands of financing, building, organizing, and broadly guiding their districts. As a result, it is no longer possible for most administrators in the central office to maintain close and continuous contact with the details of the program of instruction being carried on daily inside their individual schools. In all except the smallest districts, they can no longer know many of their teachers as individuals. Therefore, they can't keep abreast of what actually takes place within their classrooms, unless their attention is drawn by isolated examples of particularly good or bad teacher performance.

Unfortunately, few principals are in a much better position to work individually with their faculties. Even the principals of large schools, assisted as they often are by substantial staffs of vice-principals and deans, find it very difficult to provide specific guidance and direction to their teachers. Like their superintendents, principals must cope with a seemingly endless list of community and school problems. These may range from minority pressure groups in the neighborhood to student rebels on campus who wear their hair too long and their skirts too short, and from gang fights and vandalism in the playgrounds to drug trafficking in the corridors.

But it is not just these heavy and insistent demands on their time which prevent the superintendent, curriculum director, and even the principal from providing sufficient instructional leadership within the school. The complexity of the curricula in a modern school virtually precludes the possibility that any single individual can do more than manage its general direction. Typically, the high school of today will offer courses in electronics, advanced languages, world literature, calculus, ceramics, business law, modern dance, and so on through an impressive list. Obviously, no administrator can hope to remain more than broadly knowledgeable about these many and varied fields, especially in an age when each is being drastically reorganized by its own scholars. Indeed, because of the demands placed upon him by the community without and the curricula within, it might be a rare principal who could even keep up in the subject which he himself had taught before he became an administrator! As a result, the average administrator is hard-pressed to provide the necessary instructional leadership which his teachers require. According to one study, principals may in actual practice spend as little as five per cent of their time in any working week helping teachers to achieve a superior level of instruction in their classrooms.[1] This situation produces a kind of vacuum within schools, insofar as individual teachers are concerned. Locked in their daily schedules of five, six, or even more classes, shut off from the counsel of district and school administrators, these instructors can experience such a sense of isolation and drift that the effectiveness of their work is seriously impaired.

The major responsibility of the department head is to prevent this from happening. It is his task to provide the vital communications link between the administration and the teaching faculty in each subject field. It is also up to him to offer direct, on-the-spot leadership to the instructors placed under his direction. Administrators should recognize that there are several reasons why the department head is in a uniquely favorable position to meet this responsibility successfully.[2]

ASSESSING THE STRENGTHS
OF THE CHAIRMAN'S POSITION

Perhaps the most important of these is that the chairman himself is actively engaged in teaching; only a portion of his time is devoted to his administrative duties. This works to his advantage in two ways. For one, his participation in the act of teaching makes him "one of the group," a senior colleague rather than a distant authority figure. Teachers in his department are thus less apprehensive about bringing their problems to him, whether these involve planning lessons, selecting materials, coping with disciplinary challenges, or whatever.

Furthermore, the teachers know that he has to test the effectiveness of his ideas in the arena of his own classroom. When the department head speaks of successful or unsuccessful techniques, members of his department know that his counsel carries the weight of recent and first-hand experience.

Moreover, the chairman is the most accessible source of assistance for teachers in a school. Of all administrative-supervisory personnel in a district, he works with the smallest possible group of teachers who share a common concern: those within a single subject field. As a result, he is in an excellent position to provide those teachers with frequent, individualized assistance. And because he sees his teachers in a variety of situations as he works beside them throughout the school day, he is able to offer them advice which can affect their total performance as members of the school faculty.

And finally, because he does work within a single subject area, the department head has the opportunity to achieve a degree of subject matter mastery which is impossible for administrators with broader areas of responsibility. Unlike the generalist, the department head can keep abreast of local, state, and national scholarship in his field. He is thus in an excellent position to advise his teachers about the materials which they select, as well as about the methodologies which they employ to present those materials. A department chairman can guide his teachers in the selection of books which are appropriate for the objectives of their courses, as well as suitable for the interests and abilities of their students. He can also draw on his subject matter background to search out good filmstrips, slides, tapes, records, charts, models, and all the other numerous and varied kinds of instructional materials which are now available to assist teachers in virtually every subject field.

Thus, the department head, occupying a position which links administrators and teachers, plays a vital role in the operation of his school. His importance was emphasized by a number of California school administrators who were interviewed by the author as part of his study. As they perceived him, the department head is...

"...a catalyst for action in his department..." Dr. Lewis Allbee, assistant superintendent, San Francisco Unified School District,

"...a leader who can speak with teachers about the specifics of teaching..." Mr. Curtis Davis, assistant superintendent, San Jose Unified School District,

"...a teacher with some administrative functions who is the bridge between the administration and the teachers in a school..." Dr. Lloyd Bishop, principal, Claremont High School,

"...the instructional leader in his subject field..." Dr. F. Willard Robinson, principal, Beverly Hills High School,

"...the most knowledgeable individual and the most effective leader in his field that a district can get...a consultant and a resource person to the members of his

department..." Dr. Norman Loats, assistant superintendent, Newport-Mesa Unified School District.

The challenge to every school administrator is to make certain
that the department heads in the schools under his supervision live
up to the potential envisioned in these statements. With proper
direction and guidance, chairmen can become potent forces for
good within their schools. As such, they will prove to be
invaluable assistants to administrators in the work of improving
the personnel and instructional programs in those schools.

DEVELOPING THE CHAIRMAN'S JOB DESCRIPTION

Granted that department heads occupy a critically sensitive
position in their schools, how can a district's administrative staff
be certain that their departmental leadership is meeting its particular responsibilities?

A logical way to begin the task of assessing a department head's
achievements is by determining at the outset just what is expected
of him. Unless a chairman's duties are clearly defined, he may not
be aware of the kinds of services which he can and must provide
within his school. In such cases, his work may suffer as much from
lack of perspective as from any lack of ability on his own part.

How is a job description for a department head prepared?

School and district administrators should be wary of any
procedure for defining a chairman's area of responsibilities that
does not involve the chairman himself at every step. Any job
description which is drawn up neatly and quickly by a central
office committee may be incomplete or unrealistic. As a result, it
may never be accepted by the department head who is expected to
implement it, thus limiting its usefulness. On the other hand, a
document which results from the joint study and discussion of
administrators and department heads stands a much better chance
of being put into actual practice in a district's schools.

Just such a program of administrator-chairman cooperation
helped to produce the position analysis which was adopted for
department heads in the San Mateo Union High School District in
California. There, a committee composed of a principal (who was
later promoted to assistant superintendent for instruction) and
three department heads (including the author) representing differ-

ent schools and different subject fields was assigned the task of drawing up the district's first fully detailed description of the duties expected of its school chairmen.

The committee began its work by studying the results of a survey which had earlier been sent to every department head in the district. On this questionnaire, each chairman had been asked to list the specific tasks which he performed in his capacity of departmental leader. These were ranked in order of the amount of time actually devoted to each activity. The use of this preliminary survey enabled the committee to draw on the experiences of the entire staff of department heads in the district, while preparing the job description for their work. The survey form also gave each chairman an opportunity to report to the committee just which duties he felt were of greatest importance in his particular subject field and in his particular school situation.

The replies from the department heads were tabulated for frequency of response and were then grouped initially under six major categories of responsibilities:

1. Supervision of certificated personnel
2. Curriculum development and articulation
3. Meetings and conferences
4. Office operations
5. Student activities
6. Public relations

After extensive discussion, the committee refined these six areas into two major kinds of responsibility:

1. Supervision of personnel and development of curriculum,
2. Administration of departmental services.

Under these two broad headings were listed some 32 specific tasks which department heads reported that they regularly performed during the course of the academic year.

This list of duties, which district chairmen themselves recognized to be important parts of their assignment, was then circulated among chairmen in different schools and different subject areas for their evaluation. Their comments and suggestions were incorporated into a second draft document which was then reviewed by the district's council of principals. The final copy of the committee's report, embodying at that point the cooperative thinking of administrators and chairmen alike, was submitted to the district superintendent as the recommended job description for department heads in the San Mateo Union High School District. A copy of this appears in the appendix, together with representative job descriptions for chairmen drawn from other districts across the United States. The duties and responsibilities enumerated in the San Mateo job description are described in the next four chapters of this book.

A CHECK LIST FOR ADMINISTRATORS

This chapter has examined the position of the department head in a typical school situation. As we have seen, the chairman plays a vital part in determining how effectively every member of his department will be able to teach. How can administrators help their chairmen to recognize the importance of their responsibilities? The following check list offers a guide and starting point for immediate administrative action.

		Yes	No
1.	Are staff morale and teaching effectiveness unsatisfactory in any department in the school?	___	___
2.	Is the chairman of that department as effective as he should be?	___	___
3.	Does the district or school have a job description to guide the chairman?	___	___
3-A.	*If not:* Have plans been made to form a committee of administrators and chairmen to write such a job description.	___	___
3-B.	*If so:* Has the appropriate administrator reviewed the details of the job description with the chairman lately?	___	___
4.	Does the chairman know how to perform each of his duties effectively?	___	___
4-A.	Does he need direction to improve his work in teacher selection, orientation, and assignment? *(See Chapter 2 for Guidelines)*	___	___
4-B.	Does he need direction to become an effective supervisor of classroom instruction? *(See Chapter 3 for Guidelines)*	___	___

		Yes	No
4-C.	Does he need direction to become an effective leader in curriculum development? *(See Chapter 4 for Guidelines)*	—	—
4-D.	Does he need direction to become an effective manager of his department? *(See Chapter 5 for Guidelines)*	—	—

2

Improving the
Department Head's Effectiveness
in Teacher Selection,
Orientation, and Assignment

With proper administrative guidance, department chairmen can make very important contributions to their district personnel programs. They can begin their work in this vital area long before a teaching vacancy even exists in any district school. When the need for new staff is determined and applicants are invited for interviews, chairmen should continue to play a major role, helping administrators to select the best possible candidate for each position. And finally, when vacancies have been filled and contracts have been signed, department heads still have critical responsibilities to meet, as they help orient the new teachers to their duties and assign them to their classes. This chapter will trace the steps that a chairman must take to accomplish these goals effectively.

DEVELOPING THE CHAIRMEN'S PROFESSIONAL CONTACTS

The essential first step requires that department heads keep themselves active in their professional organizations. An active chairman will regularly attend conferences and institutes and will keep abreast of the latest scholarship in his field. Through these activities, he comes into direct personal contact with many excellent teachers and becomes familiar with the names of many more. Whenever the opportunity presents itself, an effective school chairman will discuss with these individuals the advantages to be gained by teaching in his particular school or district. In this way, he encourages the best of these teachers to apply for any positions which might open in the future, even if none is available at the moment. From these preliminary contacts made by department heads at professional gatherings, a district's personnel office should be able to develop a file of applications from outstanding teachers. These applications could be reviewed with the appropriate chairman as soon as an opening develops within the district.

A department head is in an excellent position to engage in recruiting activities while attending professional meetings. If he is an effective chairman, he knows his district, his school, and his curriculum thoroughly. With this fund of background information, he can assess the potential suitability of his fellow delegates for employment as teachers in his district. Administrators can help him in this work by making sure that he takes at least the following with him whenever he represents his district at a convention:

1. Materials which describe the district generally and which point up the advantages of teaching there. These should include brochures describing its location, salary policies, teaching conditions, etc.,

2. Information concerning the district's programs in the chairman's subject area. Courses of study, book lists, and lists of readily available instructional resources such as records or films are examples of such useful information that chairmen should have on hand,

3. District employment application forms.

Equipped with materials such as these, every chairman attending an institute become a potential deputy personnel officer for his district. His work thus becomes a valuable supplement to the efforts of the district's regular recruiting staff.

PARTICIPATING IN THE EMPLOYMENT INTERVIEW

When the need for new personnel has been identified and the district office has arranged to interview the most promising candidates, the appropriate chairmen should be invited to sit in. Administrators should see that chairmen read each applicant's confidential papers before the interviews, so that they will be familiar with the academic preparation, teaching experience, and professional recommendations of each.

How can a department head be of assistance to a principal or personnel director during an employment interview? He might be asked to describe the exact nature of the position which is open and relate it to the overall instructional programs in the department. Perhaps his greatest contribution, however, would come from effective use of his specialized knowledge of his subject. An administrator can use this specialized knowledge to test the applicant's own fund of information about his field, as well as his ability to teach it. The administrator might, for example, direct the chairman to ask the candidate how he would present a particular topic to a class of a specified level of ability. Or he might question the applicant about how he would handle a situation which occurs in classrooms in that particular subject area. A master teacher like the department head, who is thoroughly familiar with his subject and experience in teaching it, is best able to evaluate the applicant's responses to questions of this nature. This is where the administrator can use his chairman's specialized background to supplement his own more general knowledge of the characteristics of good teaching. The administrator can then add his department head's evaluation of the applicant to the conclusions which he himself had reached during the interview, to gain a reasonably clear picture of how successful the applicant might be as a teacher in that school.

Following each interview, the administrator should discuss the candidate with his chairman, and, if possible, they should reach a joint decision concerning his suitability. The administrator must, of course, retain the right of final decision in this matter, since he bears ultimate responsibility for the effective operation of his school. But if an administrator has been able to guide his chairmen to the point where they have become truly responsible and effective assistant leaders in the school, he would truly consider the situation very carefully before he employed an applicant over a department head's objections. If he chooses to do so, or if he fails to involve the chairman in the interview in the first place, the administrator must assume full responsibility for any inadequacies that might appear in the new teacher's work during the school year.

The department head should not be allowed to end his contributions to his school's personnel program once the employment interviews are completed and contracts have been signed. The effective chairman realizes that a new phase of his responsibilities begins at that point. The orientation of the new teachers must now start, and, in all probability, the chairman has only a few months in which to help his newcomers prepare to assume their duties. The chairman must understand that if he waits to begin this work until the opening of school, or even until the "workshop" days that might precede the actual start of the fall term, both the new teacher and his classes will suffer from insufficient preparation.

ORIENTING NEW TEACHERS TO THE DEPARTMENT

What might an administrator ask his department heads to do to assist in orienting newly-employed teachers? An effective school department head begins the work very soon after the new teacher's contract has been ratified by the district board of trustees. A good first step is a letter sent by the chairman to the newcomer, containing the chairman's welcome, his assurances that the department is looking forward to knowing and working with the new man, and his offer of help in finding suitable housing, etc., in the new community. A personal gesture such as this can do much to encourage a new teacher and to make him feel that the coming process of readjustment will be a pleasant one for him.

In addition, the department head's letter should confirm the exact schedule of classes which the new teacher will be assigned when school opens. The chairman should also ask the new instructor to prepare preliminary lesson plans for these classes during the summer and to have these ready for inspection before the opening of school. Finally, the chairman should certainly include with the letter any materials which would be useful to the new teacher as he prepares for his new assignment. Materials which are appropriate to send at this time include the following:

1.   Department courses of study,
2.   School or departmental policy statements relative to student grouping, grading, discipline, etc.
3.   Lists of books and readily available instructional resources such as records, tapes, filmstrips, slides, models, etc., within the school or department.

A beginning teacher must receive these during the spring or early summer if they are to be useful to him in preparing for his coming assignment. If they are presented to him in one large and undigestible package on the day before his classes begin, he will have no opportunity to give them the careful examination which they require.

During the summer, the department head should keep the new teacher informed of any facts which affect his assignment or the preparation of his lesson plans. There should be no unpleasant surprises awaiting the newcomer when he reports for duty in the fall!

The department head should also be directed to meet with his new teachers before the opening of school in the fall, to review their proposed lesson plans and to answer any final questions which they have about the district, the school, or their own individual situations. The author knows from experience that these queries may cover topics ranging from attendance procedures within the school to the availability of health insurance or even the quality of food in the school cafeteria! An effective department head recognizes that he performs a valuable service for his school by inviting and answering questions of such nature. The teacher with unresolved problems is not as good a teacher as he might be, and sometimes the most innocuous query may be a prelude to a serious discussion. Administrators should understand that new teachers are often hesitant to bring their personal questions to them, and so department heads must be alerted to their responsibilities in this rather delicate area of teacher orientation.

During the initial series of meetings in the fall, the chairman should also be guided to look for ways in which he can assure the new teacher that he is a valued addition to the school and department. One policy which the author has found quite effective and therefore recommends is that new teachers be allowed first choice among instructional materials available to instructors in a department. A new teacher recognizes that he is an important member of the team when he sees that he is not assigned leftover books, for example, and that even the most senior members of the department (always including the chairman himself) will adjust their own preferences to suit his plans. From this, he experiences a sense of worth which disposes him to do his best to live up to the high expectations that his colleagues have of him.

The orientation process is not completed with the opening of school. Throughout the year, chairmen should be asked to meet periodically with their new teachers, to discuss school and departmental policies and practices. Some of the items to be considered at these meetings might be suggested by school or district administrators, to supplement the information which they present in their own orientation programs. Other topics could come from experienced members of the department, who should be invited to join the meetings as resource persons, or from teachers in the department who were newcomers themselves only a year or two earlier. Of course, additional subjects to discuss should be suggested by the new teachers themselves; the effective department head invites and welcomes such cooperative participation.

From this summary, it can be seen that department heads with proper guidance and training can become key figures in a district's personnel development program. Administrators can capitalize on each chairman's potential value to this program by establishing a calendar of specific activities in which department heads are asked to participate. These activities should proceed in logical sequence from making contacts at professional conferences through involvement in employment interviews and then on into the follow-up letters and meetings which are essential for effective teacher orientation.

UNDERSTANDING THE SIGNIFICANCE
OF TEACHING ASSIGNMENTS

School department heads have one more critically important responsibility in the areas of staff development and utilization: preparing their departmental teaching schedules.

Administrators must recognize that the chairman's decisions in this part of his work touch on a highly sensitive area for most teachers. Therefore, each chairman should receive careful direction when he prepares his teachers' assignments. Furthermore, his recommendations must be reviewed carefully by the appropriate administrator in the school or district, to make certain that they fairly and efficiently utilize the strengths of each member of his department and that they provide for the continuous professional development of every teacher. This part of the chapter will show why such careful administrative review is essential and will recommend guidelines for administrators and chairmen alike.

For a variety of reasons, teachers are very concerned about the kinds of classes which they are assigned to teach. They wish, of course, to work in areas where they are well prepared and comfortably secure in their mastery of the material to be covered. A department head can cause his teachers a great deal of anxiety if he ignores this fact and schedules them to instruct classes where they are not thoroughly familiar with the subject. The reason for this is simple. Today's students form a highly critical audience and are often quick to reject the teacher whose performance does not meet their standards. An instructor in such a situation faces at least a year of unrewarding drudgery; he may also have to contend with major disciplinary problems among his students.

There is also a strong element of teacher prestige and even of teacher self-identification involved in the matter of classroom assignments. Teachers are denied the ego satisfaction of outward symbols of status, so long as they remain in their classrooms and do not seek administrative positions. Teachers are not ordinarily distinguished from each other by titles which proclaim degrees of proficiency, as do the professorial ranks found in most colleges. Neither do they wear insignia of rank such as academic robes with differentiated markings. Teacher salaries, of course, do reflect differences in preparation and experience, but administrators can recall from their own experiences that there is little gratification to be found in announcing that one has achieved column four on the salary schedule, representing the bachelor's degree plus 45 units. There does exist some distinction between the tenured and the probationary teacher, but achieving tenure status confers precious little by way of enduring prestige.

Denied these traditional sources of job status, teachers often seek to derive distinction from the kinds of classes which they usually teach. Thus, administrators may be very familiar with "the senior teacher" or "the honors teacher," types which manifest themselves in many departments in a school. At the same time, an instructor who is scheduled to work with a remedial class or two may be categorized by some of his colleagues as "the basic skills teacher," with the implication that his own intelligence and interests are on a level with those of his students.

It should be clear, therefore, that teachers attach great importance to their assignments. Administrators should properly delegate the responsibility of preparing these schedules to their chairmen, for they are most familiar with the subject field and with the individual talents and personalities of their teachers. At the same time, however, department heads should receive careful guidance in carrying out this task.

PREPARING TEACHING ASSIGNMENTS—
THE WRONG AND RIGHT WAYS

By manipulating his department's schedule, an unprofessional chairman can maintain a morale-destroying tyranny within his department, punishing critics of his policies and rewarding sycophantic followers. If administrators do not review recommended assignments carefully, such a department head might give five or six remedial classes to a beginner or to a potential rival, while reserving more "choice" assignments for himself and his friends. He can also deliberately assign teachers to classes for which they have little preparation or assign them an impossible variety of classes for which to prepare daily. Such a chairman might also keep his department's class schedule a private secret until the opening of school, in order to enjoy a sense of power as "keeper of the mysteries." Unfortunately, this list of possible abuses of a department head's authority in the area of preparing teaching assignments could be extended even further, as many teachers can testify.

On the other hand, a conscientious department head who has received proper training and direction proceeds in a more professional and democratic manner. He consults his colleagues in advance of preparing the departmental teaching schedule, to be sure that he knows the kinds of classes with which each teacher wants to work. He might well ask them to draw up a kind of ideal daily schedule for themselves, showing the classes which they like to teach in each period of the school day and also showing their preferences for a preparation or activity period. Such a chairman weighs his teachers' expressed wishes carefully when he assigns their programs.

Chairmen must be guided to do more than simply consult their colleagues when they draw up their departmental schedules, however. The effective school department head will play a highly creative role in staff development when he assigns classes.

Such a chairman will utilize his knowledge of his subject area and of his teachers' talents and personalities to develop a schedule which will improve their professional abilities and performances. He can do this by establishing larger classes to be taught by teams of instructors, each working in a preferred area, but all carefully matched so that the strengths of one compensate for the weaknesses of another. In such a situation, the instructors have an opportunity to learn from each other and thus to remedy their own deficiencies. For example, a teacher who is highly creative but whose work is hampered by an inability to organize or control a class could be teamed with another who is more methodical in his approach but who is always in effective control of his classes. Both instructors would benefit from this arrangement.

Moreover, a good chairman encourages teachers who have become too comfortably entrenched in familiar subject areas to accept at least one new course periodically, to help them remain professionally competent and intellectually stimulated by their work. On the other hand, the effective chairman is alert to counsel teachers against seeking assignments for which they lack suitable preparation, either academic or psychological. He also makes certain that the department's "plum" and "pill" courses are fairly distributed, to prevent any teacher from becoming stereotyped or stigmatized by his assignments.

Administrators should also guide their chairmen to weigh their choice of classes for themselves just as thoughtfully when they draw up their departmental schedules. As a general rule, a department head's own program should cover the spectrum of subjects taught in his department, insofar as the degree of specialization required for each course permits. Even if a chairman feels himself to be best qualified to teach in the more advanced classes in his department, he should also assign himself at least one elementary section each year.

Administrators can point out that there are several benefits to be derived by chairmen who adopt such a policy of assigning themselves a broad range of classes. For one, it will save them from any charges that they have hoarded their departments' more desirable classes for themselves. This alone strengthens a chairman's position among his colleagues and increases the likelihood of his being accepted by them as a truly professional leader, worthy of their respect and support. Moreover, by periodically changing at least a part of his own assignment, the department head keeps himself in closer touch with all levels of his department. This enables him to speak with greater knowledge and authority concerning all aspects of his program. The great strength of an effective department head lies in the fact that he is truly a link between administrators and every teacher in his department. He must understand, therefore, that this requires that he work alongside all of his colleagues, teaching all levels of his subject field with them.

When departmental programs have finally been prepared, chairmen should be instructed to discuss them with every member of their staffs before they are submitted to the appropriate administrator in the school or district. In this way, any improvements which could be made are identified at the departmental level and accomplished there. Finally, any changes which have to be made in a recommended schedule in order to fit it to the school's master program must be communicated to the teachers involved by the chairman, so that they will have time to adjust their plans accordingly.

A CHECK LIST FOR ADMINISTRATORS

In this chapter, we have traced the ways in which an effective school department head can help in his district's program of teacher selection, orientation, and assignment. The following checklist will help administrators to evaluate the performance of their department heads in each of these important areas of responsibility.

		Yes	No
1.	Has each chairman attended at least one professional conference or institute in the past three years?	___	___
2.	Did every chairman have a package of teacher recruitment materials to take with him to the conference?	___	___
3.	Did every chairman report back the name of at least one possible candidate for employment whom he had contacted at the conference?	___	___
4.	Does every department head participate effectively in interviews with teacher candidates?	___	___
5.	Does every chairman provide lesson planning materials for new teachers during the summer?	___	___
6.	Do chairmen meet with new teachers before the opening of school?	___	___
7.	Do chairmen meet periodically with new teachers after the opening of school?	___	___
8.	Does every chairman understand how important a fair and efficient teaching assignment is to staff morale?	___	___
9.	Were all teachers consulted regarding their choice of classes before departmental programs were prepared?	___	___
10.	If teachers were assigned to classes other than those which they requested, were there sound reasons for the changes, and were they fully explained to the teachers involved?	___	___

Yes   *No*

11. Do departmental schedules utilize the strengths of some teachers to offset the weaknesses of others?   ___ ___

12. Do departmental schedules encourage professional growth among teachers by expanding the range of classes which they usually teach?   ___ ___

13. Do departmental schedules fairly distribute classes of greater and lesser desirability among all teachers, while taking into account their interests and abilities?   ___ ___

14. Does each chairman's choice of classes for himself contribute to developing his capabilities as departmental leader?   ___ ___

15. Are all necessary changes in departmental schedules communicated to the teachers involved?   ___ ___

3

Establishing the Department Head as an Effective Classroom Supervisor

Are department heads line or staff personnel?

The effective school department head welcomes the opportunity to work with his teachers—as a consultant. In this capacity, he helps them to plan units, select materials, and design strategies. He sees this as his most important contribution to improving their classroom performance. Most chairmen, however, dread the responsibility of having to follow-up their work by observing their teachers in their classrooms, to evaluate the effectiveness of their performance. But, if chairmen are to be truly effective assistants to their principals, they must serve as both consultants and supervisors for the teachers in their departments.

In this chapter, administrators will find a practical, operational program designed to help their department heads reconcile their two essential roles and become better classroom supervisors. Guidelines will be offered to show chairmen why they must supervise regular and substitute teachers in their subject areas—and how they can do it effectively.

41

Why is supervision such a difficult task for most chairmen? Typically, a good department head minimizes the authoritarian aspects of his position in his work with his colleagues. He avoids actions which seem to be arbitrary in nature or which seem to manipulate personnel and policy. Instead, he works to develop within his department an open, democratic atmosphere in which all teachers have an opportunity to share their ideas and experiences freely. Such a chairman is most often found in the department office or faculty rooms engaged in frank discussions with his colleagues, debating the theory and practice of good teaching in a give and take manner which encourages others to express their own viewpoints.

Inevitably, however, department heads must all face the responsibility of helping to provide effective supervision of instruction within the classrooms of their departments. Administrators recognize that there is no substitute for such first-hand observation. A teacher may present the most detailed and promising lesson plans for approval; principals and supervisors know from experience that these plans may or may not be successfully implemented in that teacher's room the next day. Another instructor may discuss his classroom performance in the most glowing terms over a cup of coffee with his chairman, describing how intently his students had hung on his every word during the electrifying hour just completed. But again, administrators know from their own training and experience that what a teacher perceives from the front of his room is not always what actually occurs in the back of the room, behind the first few rows of students.

Consequently, successful administrators know that an impartial, objective observer of a teacher's classroom performance is able to offer that teacher valuable insights which can help him to improve his lesson planning and presentation. The effective school department head recognizes this fact and acts accordingly. Far from dreading the responsibility for providing classroom supervision, he knows that supervision which is carried on properly will in no way compromise his position as colleague and consultant in his department. For, as one superintendent put it:

"The word 'supervision' has attracted so many unfavorable connotations that it may be hard to realize that it denotes coordination, stimulation (as well as) evaluation...its purposes...

include welding teachers into an effective team in the achievement of agreed-upon objectives, releasing the unique talents of the staff, inducting new teachers into the educational enterprise, translating theory into practice, furnishing help with 'housekeeping' difficulties, motivating teachers to enlarge their cultural horizons, helping teachers to evaluate their teaching, aiding the staff in necessary planning, discovering needed changes and recommending changes necessary for improvement, upgrading content mastery, improving teaching methods, acquainting teachers with new developments and resources, helping in the evaluation of pupils, communicating problems and successes to...administrators and community representatives, and most of all, developing a professional esprit de corps among the...staff."[3]

SOLVING THE CHAIRMAN'S DILEMMA

Unfortunately, however, most teachers view the presence of an observer in their classrooms with some uneasiness. They use the epithet "snoopervisor" to describe the unwanted or mistrusted classroom visitor. The cause for their concern is quite simple.

During the actual process of teaching, an instructor reveals most clearly his personal and professional strengths or weaknesses. And he knows that in-class supervision, however expertly his department head may conduct it, is inextricably linked with evaluation of those strengths and weaknesses. The chairman may work hard to establish an open, cooperative spirit of professionalism within his department, but when he observes his teachers in their classrooms, he will be perceived by them as an administrative deputy. They know that administrators confer with their chairman regarding matters of teacher assignment, tenure, and promotion, and reports of classroom performance will weigh heavily in those conferences.

The problem then remains: how may a department head practice in-class supervision without jeopardizing the positive relationships which he has developed with his teacher-colleagues? This problem is not easily solved. The author knows of many chairmen who have found it impossible to reconcile these conflicting responsibilities and who have either resigned their positions or simply given up making classroom observations.

Neither of these courses of action can be acceptable to the chairman's administrative superiors. The first may remove the best qualified and most capable teacher from the post where he is urgently needed. The second places upon the school administration the entire responsibility of providing evaluative leadership among teachers in a particular subject field. And as we noted earlier, the principal and his assistants may have neither the time nor the specialized training necessary to accomplish this. Furthermore, the author would question the justification for retaining a good teacher in a department head position if he chooses to limit his responsibilities to essentially managerial functions.

When a department head does accept the responsibilities of observation and evaluation, how can he work in such a way that his classroom visitations will be as helpful and "painless" as possible for his teachers? Administrators who wish to guide their chairmen in this critically sensitive area might recommend the following procedures.

DEVELOPING AN EFFECTIVE VISITATION PROGRAM

The department head should begin by making classroom visitation such a common practice in his department that it loses its novelty and thus, to some degree, its threatening aspect. The chairman can do this by scheduling each of his teachers (both new and experienced) to visit at least one other class in the department each semester. This policy provides valuable in-service training to the entire department by making it possible for instructors to observe at first-hand the materials and techniques which their colleagues use in their classrooms. Parenthetically, the chairman will undoubtedly encourage his teachers to accept this policy if he makes it quite clear that his own classes are as open for observation as anyone else's.

By involving so many people in the act of visiting classes or receiving visitors themselves, the department head shows his colleagues that making observations is not just an administrative practice, reserved for those who are assigned to supervise the performance of others. Instead, it is a very valuable learning practice for observer and observed alike. Moreover, a teacher who has already observed and been observed half a dozen times in a department where such a policy of inter-class visitation prevails will not feel nervous when the latest visitor happens to be the chairman himself.

As a second step in a program designed to provide effective classroom supervision, the department head should plan to conduct his own visits in a variety of ways. He must understand that teachers cannot be fairly evaluated on the basis of just one or two "official" observations in their classes. All teachers have had successful days, and all teachers have had days during which a visitor would merely have been one more calamity to be added to an already long list of disasters. Therefore, the department head must see his teachers in many different situations if he is to judge their work accurately and make proper recommendations to them and to school administrators.

One way to be sure that teachers are seen at their best is to encourage them to invite their chairman into their classes when something is happening which they particularly want him to observe. Watching a teacher present a lesson of which he himself is proud will give the chairman a good estimate of that teacher's potential for excellence. And visiting a room when students are demonstrating the successful end of a unit of work through panel discussions, project displays, or similar activities will enable the chairman to evaluate how well that potential was realized.

Of course, the department head should also enter classes from time to time when he is not specifically expected. An effective department head exercises discretion in making these unscheduled visitations. He will not arrive on the heels of a football rally which has left the students unusually agitated or on the first day of school after a lengthy vacation, when students might be expected to appear unusually lethargic. The chairman should also display the same degree of courtesy to the teacher in front of the class that he himself would expect in that position: his arrival and exit should be as unobtrusive as possible, and his own actions or expressions should in no way distract or intimidate the teacher. These un-announced classroom visitations should also be varied in length. The first might last just a few minutes each, allowing the department head to note the overall atmosphere of the class, the teacher's general plans and procedures, and the room's characteristics. Before evaluations are finally made, however, the chairman should plan to spend at least one entire class period with each of his teachers (more for those who require additional assistance), arriving before the students enter the room and leaving after they have departed.

HOLDING FOLLOW-UP CONFERENCES WITH TEACHERS

Regardless of the length and frequency of the department head's visits to his teachers' classes, he has one final responsibility to discharge in order to become an effective classroom supervisor. He must find an opportunity within a day or so of each visit to confer individually with the teacher whom he has observed, if his observations are truly to be for the purpose of giving instructional aid and advice. A chairman who does not conduct such follow-up conferences may leave the teachers concerned with mistaken impressions of how he reacted to their work. Such silence can induce acute anguish in a new or insecure teacher. One may wonder if a supervisor ever accomplishes much that is worthwhile by visiting a class and then not following through with a conference with the teacher involved. Indeed, the author questions whether a supervisor who frequently omits such conferences should have the right to continue to make classroom visitations.

Even under the best of circumstances, however, discussions between a supervisor and a teacher whose class has been visited will require careful handling. The teacher can be expected to feel somewhat defensive in such a situation and might not be receptive to evaluations and recommendations made by his department head. Consequently, the chairman must be given appropriate guidance from his administrative superiors if these conferences are to result in a worthwhile exchange of information and opinions.

Administrators might direct their department heads to begin each of these follow-up meetings with their teachers by asking the instructor involved to discuss the objectives which had guided his work with the class during the period in which the observation took place. This kind of introduction helps to relieve the teacher of any anxiety which he might be feeling. He is given the opportunity of making the initial statements in the discussion, to explain his situation and his intentions as fully as he wishes. Most importantly, however, this technique allows the department head and the teacher to establish the framework in which a truly objective, professional discussion can take place. Thus, if the teacher defines his objective as having been X, then the chairman proceeds logically when he discusses that objective in light of departmental programs and student needs and abilities. And he maintains this professional objectivity when he evaluates the methods and materials which the teacher had used to achieve his objective during the class hour. Throughout the meeting, this practice of evaluating in terms of specified objectives makes possible the kind of systematic, controlled discussion which is most likely to result in real learning occurring on the part of the teacher—and sometimes of the chairman as well!

Administrators should also instruct their department heads to keep two additional points in mind while they confer with their teachers after visiting their classrooms. Perhaps rather obviously, the conferences ought never be totally negative in tone or content, regardless of the kind of performance which was just observed. It is a rare teacher who can't be praised for something in his methods or materials, and pointing out even this one commendable quality helps to prepare the teacher for any less positive comments that might have to follow.

Moreover, the department head should be reminded to make careful notes on the specific points covered in the conference. Included in these notes should be the following information:

1. Exact details concerning the situation in which the classroom observation was made, including the date, hour, and length of the observation, the nature of the class visited, and whether that class had been visited previously,

2. A summary of what occurred within the classroom during the period of the observation,

3. An evaluation of the specific strengths and weaknesses of the teacher's performance or the class's procedures as noted during the course of the observation,

4. Any general or specific recommendations offered for improving the teacher's work in the future.

After he has had a chance to put these notes into readable form, the chairman should prepare at least three copies of them. The teacher concerned should be asked to sign each copy of the report, indicating that its contents are accurate and have been discussed with him. He should also have the opportunity to add information of his own to the report, if he so desires. One copy should then go to the teacher for his future reference, another to the department head's administrative superior, and a third should be kept in the chairman's own files. In any future conference involving this particular teacher, the notes of previous discussions could thus be consulted by each participant, and all would have a basis for evaluating the progress made by the teacher in improving his performance. This procedure is useful in helping a good teacher to develop his talents even further. It is essential in preparing a case for dismissal against a poor teacher, particularly in states which have adopted rigidly binding tenure laws.

SUPERVISING SUBSTITUTE TEACHERS
AND STUDENT TEACHERS

Besides supervising the regular teachers in his department, the chairman must also be prepared to work with substitute teachers or student teachers whenever such personnel are assigned to his department. Every chairman should be guided in formulating specific plans and procedures for providing these people with classroom assistance as the need arises.

Substitutes for regular teachers who are ill from time to time may require a great deal of help from their department head. He may be asked to assist the school administration in orienting substitutes to the school and to their assigned classes. The chairman may also prove to be a valuable "trouble-shooter" when substitutes run into difficulties—as they so often do.

As his contribution to the process of orientation, the department head can describe the kinds of classes which the substitutes will work with and can help them to find their way about the school. The chairman also provides additional help when he explains attendance and discipline policies, library procedures, and so forth. He should also arrange to meet briefly with the substitutes between classes or at lunch, to review their progress and to offer such additional help as they may require.

A department head can be of most help in supervising substitute teachers when unexpected problems occur and the chairman is called upon to act as an emergency "trouble-shooter." A cool head and a sound knowledge of his department's programs and staff are a chairman's most valuable assets at such moments. He may be asked to track down missing keys for classroom doors, unearth lesson plans left buried in piles of papers on the absent teachers' desks, or even to improvise lesson plans on the spot when none can be found. In extreme situations, a department head must also be prepared to rescue a substitute teacher from a classroom crisis and to take over the teaching of that class for the remainder of the period.

What can an effective school department head do to minimize the problems that might confront substitute teachers in his department? Administrators should ask their chairmen to take at least the following precautionary steps:

1. Frequently remind all teachers in the department to leave their classroom keys and lesson plans in a designated, readily accessible place whenever they anticipate the possibility of being absent from school.

2. Require each teacher to prepare an "emergency lesson plan" for each of his classes, to be filed in the department office or the chairman's own classroom. These would be used in the event that a sudden illness or accident prevented a teacher from making the necessary advance preparations for being absent. Such plans as these should outline an essentially self-contained, single-day unit of study or activity which could be presented at any point in the school year and which would be worthwhile for the students involved. The chairman will probably find it useful to have just such a plan or two of his own on hand for use whenever he has to relieve a subsitute teacher of a class and finds that the existing lesson plan for the day is unsatisfactory.

3. Keep a master key for all the classrooms in his

department, filed in a secure place in the department office or in his own classroom.

In addition to supervising substitute teachers when they are
assigned to his department, the chairman must also be ready to
work with student or cadet teachers who may be placed in his
department from a nearby college. As a master teacher, the
department head bears a special responsibility for the young
college men and women who are receiving their teacher training in
his subject field and in his school.

The effective department head will meet this responsibility
initially by recommending that student teachers be assigned to
work only with the best instructors in his department. He avoids
the temptation to place a promising cadet in the classroom of a
substandard teacher, so that the beginner's talents might improve
an otherwise mediocre teaching situation. Such a practice is sheer
exploitation of the cadet, requiring that he give to his training
experience much more than he receives from it.

After the initial successful placement is accomplished, the
department head probably will need to do little but confer
occasionally with the student teacher and the supervising teacher,
to see that they are working well together and to offer whatever
assistance they might require. If the supervising teacher reports
that the beginner is doing a particularly good job, the department
head might observe the class a few times personally. If his own
observation confirms the teacher's reports, the chairman should
invite his administrative superior to visit the student teacher for
additional confirmation and should send the cadet's name to the
district personnel office, to be listed among potentially desirable
candidates for future employment in the district. On the other
hand, if the beginner's performance indicates that he probably will
never develop into even an adequate teacher, the chairman can
expect to be called in to validate this judgment. He might then
have to assist the supervising teacher in the delicate task of
suggesting that the cadet seek elsewhere for a profession.

Finally, in his capacity as classroom supervisior, the department
head is responsible for the overall progress of students who enroll
in the classrooms within his jurisdiction. Those students are, of
course, primarily the concern of their own teachers. The chairman
as an individual has fulfilled his essential obligation to them when

he has helped their teachers to improve the instructional programs which they offer in their separate classrooms.

It remains the department head's duty, however, to provide direction and coordination for student achievement in his department. He does this by examining his teachers' grade reports to insure that the students are making reasonable progress in their studies. He also does this by seeing that students are placed in classes which are most appropriate for their needs and abilities. And he accomplishes this again when he sponsors or directs programs which are designed to enrich the educational experiences of students in his department. Such programs might include departmental-related contests, conferences, or trips.

In each of these activities, the department head usually deals with pupils in their classrooms only indirectly; his principal contacts will be with administrators, counselors, and teachers in his department. Yet the chairman's direction provides an essential—if indirect—form of classroom supervision in each instance. Without this supervision, the progress of students enrolled in his department or participating in his department's program of activities will not be as great as it could be.

A CHECK LIST FOR ADMINISTRATORS

This chapter has outlined the reasons why chairmen must supervise classroom teaching in their departments. In addition, a program designed to help chairmen practice classroom supervision effectively has been recommended for administrative implementation. The check list which follows will provide a profile of the present effectiveness of a school's department heads in meeting their responsibilities in this area.

		Yes	No
1.	Does each department head understand and accept his responsibility to supervise classroom teaching in his subject area?	——	——
2.	Does each department have a policy of encouraging and scheduling regular inter-class visitations among its teachers?	——	——
3.	Does each chairman encourage his teachers to invite him into their classrooms?	——	——

		Yes	No
4.	Does each chairman also visit classes in his department on an unschedules basis?	___	___
5.	Are these visitations conducted with proper concern for the teacher and students in each room?	___	___
6.	Is each visitation followed by a conference with the teacher concerned?	___	___
7.	Are these conferences conducted in a constructive, professional manner?	___	___
8.	Is a complete and accurate report prepared on each visitation and conference, with copies properly distributed?	___	___
9.	Has each chairman made specific, detailed plans for minimizing the classroom problems which substitute teachers might encounter in his department?	___	___
10.	Does each chairman understand and fulfill his responsibilities in assigning and supervising student teachers?	___	___
11.	Does each chairman regularly monitor the progress of students enrolled in classrooms in his department?	___	___

4

The Department Head
as an Effective Leader
in Curriculum Development

Administrators are ultimately responsible for the instructional programs which are offered in their schools and districts. If these programs are to be as vital and current as our complex world now requires, administrators will need to draw on the specialized training and experience of their department heads to design the curriculum for each subject area. This chapter will recommend ways in which administrators can guide their chairmen to become curriculum leaders in their individual fields. The role and functions of the effective school department head will be traced as he helps to establish instructional objectives in his department and then assists his teachers in acquiring the ideas, skills, and materials which they will need to accomplish those objectives.

As indicated, the essential first step is to define the objectives of each department's instructional programs. How can administrators guide their chairmen as they undertake this task? Unless the administrator is himself an expert in a particular department's subject field, he may feel that his own role and contribution will of necessity be quite limited. Actually, however, he can provide valuable overall direction for each chairman by taking the following actions

53

1. He can establish and supervise the procedures by which the department will define its objectives. Applying appropriate management techniques, the administrator can see that a sound and logical sequence of activities is established and followed in each department. These activities should involve the total staff in each subject area, under the chairman's direction, and should be tied to a time table which will insure that reasonable and consistent progress will be made in each department toward accomplishing its task.

2. The administrator can utilize his broad perspective of the total school or district programs to examine the objectives developed in each department. He can assess their usefulness and appropriateness in light of a variety of criteria:

    A. Educational philosophies and curriculum policies already established for the state, district, and school,

    B. Educational needs, as revealed in follow-up studies of the success or failure of school and district graduates who have sought entry into colleges and occupations in the area,

    C. Recommendations made by civic, business, and educational leaders in the area or as reported in current research studies.

3. He can apply the principles of systems analysis to curriculum development by making certain that departmental objectives are tested and that the results of those tests are used to continuously refine the objectives.

4. Finally, Where the administrator finds similar objectives present in several departments, he can encourage the chairmen and teachers in those departments to work together to develop interdisciplinary programs which will coordinate their efforts to achieve those objectives.

Operating within these administrative guidelines, the individual department head can now begin to provide curriculum leadership in his particular subject area.

A chairman may designate grade level or subject coordinators within his department to assist him in the task of curriculum development. Or he may ask particular teachers to assume responsibility for specialized tasks such as developing instructional materials for use by the entire group. Regardless of the degree of assistance which he may receive from his teachers, however, the department head must recognize that the development of his department's curriculum remains primarily his own responsibility.

He must realize that individual teachers who carry full teaching loads cannot be expected to assume direction of an overall program of which their own classroom programs constitute a part. These instructors may work very had to improve their individual performances in their classrooms, but the leadership which establishes the general departmental curriculum must come from the chairman himself. The effective school department head recognizes this fact, but he also understands that he must involve his colleagues at every step in the process of curriculum development if he expects them to support and implement the final product.

The effective school department head gives initial impetus to the process of curriculum development within his subject area by asking his staff to help define the kind of educational product which they want their programs to produce. This is the vital first step toward defining the objectives of the department's instruction. Operating within the administrative guidelines discussed earlier, the chairman will insist that these objectives be stated as specifically as possible.

The department must not be content to construct noble but vague generalities for its goals because it is usually impossible to determine whether such goals are ever really met. Of course, the case can be made that the ultimate goal of all education is "to prepare students to live full, meaningful lives which provide personal satisfaction by enabling them to participate actively and creatively in their society." But no school or department can expect such a goal to provide necessary guidelines for assessing the effectiveness of the instructional programs which it offers. Instead, each department must determine what kinds of specific, measurable objectives its students will need to reach in order to live such optimum lives. Then it will have to design a curriculum leading toward the accomplishment of those objectives.

DEVELOPING PERFORMANCE OBJECTIVES

But how does a department set about the task of developing instructional objectives which are stated in terms of measurable criteria performances? Administrators might recommend for their department heads' guidance the operational plan outlined below. This plan was developed and implemented recently in the author's own department, and it may serve as a possible example, if not a model.

The first step in the author's plan was to explain to teachers in his department exactly why performance objectives are worth writing down in the first place. The possible benefits to be derived from defining objectives in terms of measurable performances were listed as follows:

1.   Both teachers and students will have a clearer understanding of *why* they study a particular unit or engage in a particular activity when they have a clearer conception of *what* goals they are working toward.

2.   Teachers will be able to use more varied and individualized instructional techniques and materials when they have made their instructional goals more specific.

3.   Teachers and students alike will be able to determine how well they have succeeded in reaching their instructional objectives when those goals are stated in specific, measurable terms. In the event that they are not successful on one attempt, teachers and students will be able to work more cooperatively to revise instructional procedures so as to come closer to success on the next attempt.

The next step was to establish a specific and manageable plan for actually writing the objectives. The author's department followed this procedure:

1. Preparation

A. A small number of teachers with related backgrounds of classroom experience formed a writing committee to draft the first set of objectives. Five teachers served on the committee; the author sat in on their meetings from time to time to provide guidance and support.

B. Released time for three full school days was provided for the group through the district's teacher executive program. (See Chapter 9 for details of this innovative program.)

C. Conference space and working materials and resources were provided for the group. These resources included a number of background reading selections dealing with performance objectives and extracts from *Taxonomy of Educational Objectives, Handbook I: Cognitive Domain*, edited by Benjamin S. Bloom (New York: David McKay, Inc., 1956). For specific direction, a worksheet with the following headings was provided for the writing of each performance objective:

Students in What Kind of Class?	Given What Time, Materials, and Environment?	Will Do What?	With What Degree of Accuracy or Excellence?

2. Development

A. The committee, with the cooperation and guidance of the entire department, then decided upon answers to four important questions:

(1) For what specific courses would the performance objectives be written?

(2) For what specific parts of the instructional program within those courses (i.e. literature, composition, etc.) would the performance objectives be written?

(3) For what levels (from Bloom's *Taxonomy*) would the performance objectives be written?

(4) How many performance objectives would be written?

B. With these guidelines established, and following the questions specified on their work sheets, the teacher group proceeded to write the performance objectives. Each of these has the following characteristics:

(1) It says what a student who has achieved the objective will be able to do.

(2) It specifies the conditions under which the student will be able to do what is asked of him.

(3) It states how well the student will be able to do the desired action; that is, it specifies the minimum standard of acceptable performance.

(4) It indicates how the performance will be evaluated.

3. Evaluation and Implementation

A. The performance objectives developed by the committee were reviewed by the department as a whole, to determine whether they were valid and appropriate instructional goals.

B. The performance objectives were then tested in the classes for which they were designed.

(1) At the beginning of the semester, the students in the classes were informed of the objectives which they would be asked to master.

(2) To the extent that the teachers of those classes so desired, the students were invited to help plan the instructional program which led up to their accomplishing the specified objectives.

(3) Periodic tests were administered throughout the semester, to monitor student progress toward achieving the goals.

(4) Final performance tests were administered at the end of the semester.

C. On the basis of the results of the final performance tests, the objectives were reviewed by the department, and necessary additional revisions were made. This process of testing and revision on the basis of "feedback" results continued regularly thereafter.

The above procedure was repeated the following year, with development of another small group of terminal performance objectives to be added to those already adopted by the department. In this way, the department has slowly and carefully produced a small bank of teacher-constructed and teacher-validated performance objectives for every course which it offers.

It should be emphasized in conclusion that only terminal

(end of semester) performance objectives were developed within the author's department. No attempt was made to establish department-wide goals for shorter units of study, so that teachers would be able to retain the highest possible degree of individual freedom in choosing the materials and techniques which they judged to be most suitable for meeting the varied individual differences present in their classrooms. As the author summarized in one memorandum to his colleagues:

"We have begun by specifying some of the things that we want to accomplish through our teaching. These are terminal objectives, representing critically important skills and information which we believe our students have to master by the end of each semester. Now that we have a clearer view of what we have to achieve with our classes, we will be in a much better position to analyze what we should teach, and how, and on what levels. We can begin to look at teaching as a process or system, with certain clearly definable components such as environments (indoor and outdoor spaces to be used for large and small group activities), materials (including learner activity packages and student-operated multi-media instructional systems), and instructional patterns (ranging from traditional larger lecture-discussion classes to seminar, practice, and independent study sections). And we will discover that we can exercise a large measure of deliberate, selective control over many of these components, altering their arrangements or increasing or decreasing the resources (time or money) which we commit to each, in the ways best calculated to help us reach our goals.

"Performance objectives give us a greater measure of creative freedom than we have ever been able to enjoy because they free us from the dead weight of traditional practices which may no longer be effective. Each of us will continue to teach in the way that best utilizes his individual talents, but we will all teach more effectively than ever because we will now become more skillful managers of the learning systems which operate in our classrooms.

"I hold this to be the essence of a truly professional status for the classroom teacher."

An example of the performance objectives developed in the author's department appears on page 60. Although its content is specifically related to instruction in English, its structure is readily adaptable to use in any subject area.

Once a department has established the objectives of its instruc-

ENGLISH DEPARTMENT—Performance Objective in Composition

English 3

Given:

A short story:

not to exceed 2000 words

appropriate reading level

not taught before in the class

An introductory paragraph which contains a commitment or thesis sentence

A choice of eight topic sentences:

six relevant to the commitment sentence

two not relevant to the commitment sentence

Two hours (or one hour, if the story is read before the test period)

Students Will:

Underline the commitment sentence in the given introductory paragraph

Select three of the relevant topic sentences

Write a paragraph from each of the topic sentences:

writing them so that they will follow and support the given introductory paragraph

using specific examples from the story to support the topic sentence and bracketing such examples for quick identification

avoiding irrelevant information

giving coherence to the paragraphs by *either* using transitional devices *or* repeating the idea stated in the commitment sentence, so that the paragraphs are logically linked

underlining the transitional devices or the words which repeat the idea stated in the commitment sentence

writing in complete sentences

With These Minimum Standards:

The correct commitment sentence must be chosen; choice of an incorrect commitment sentence will fail the paper

All topic sentences chosen must be relevant to the commitment sentence; choice of an irrelevant topic sentence will fail the paper

Each paragraph must contain at least one specific example from the story to support the topic sentence; failure to include such a specific example will fail the paragraph

Each paragraph must not have more than one sentence fragment or run-on sentence; the presence of more than one of either will fail the paragraph

Irrelevant information must be excluded from each paragraph; the presence of such information will fail the paragraph

Each paragraph must show its coherence with the entire composition by containing underlined transitional devices or the underlined restatement of the main idea from the commitment sentence given in the introductory paragraph; failure to use such connective techniques will fail the paragraph

* * * * * * * * * * * * * * *

Failure of any one paragraph will pass the paper; failure of any two paragraphs will fail the paper

tional programs, it is ready to develop the component parts of its curriculum, to help students to achieve the specified goals. A large part of the time scheduled for department meetings should be reserved for curriculum production and revision. In addition, the department might subdivide itself into task groups which meet periodically, perhaps at noon or after school, to continue to work on specific parts of its curriculum. Summer workshops also provide an excellent opportunity for carrying on this kind of activity; the author knows from experience that a great deal can be accomplished when teachers have the time to meet together for extended periods of time during the summer, when they are free from the demands of their daily class preparations.

What is the chairman's role in these departmental efforts? Obviously, he should play an active and continuous part throughout, participating in committee work when desirable and appropriate, and providing liaison among the different groups at all times. There are also several important additional contributions which only the chairman can make. The effective school department head provides leadership in developing his department's curriculum in the following ways:

1. He helps his teachers to keep abreast of the most recent developments in philosophies, practices and materials in his subject area, so that his department's instructional programs will be as current and relevant as possible. Some of this necessary information he may provide personally by serving as a resource consultant for his colleagues. Professional institutes and conferences also provide an opportunity for teachers to keep up in their fields; the chairman must help his teachers to get the most benefit from attending such meetings.

2. He provides an opportunity for his teachers to exchange ideas based on their own teaching experiences. This kind of practical, "how-to-do-it-better" information is extremely stimulating and helpful in curriculum development work.

3. He involves his colleagues in the selection of books and other materials which they will use to implement and test their newly-developed curriculum.

4.   He works with grade schools and colleges to make sure that his department's curriculum is effectively articulated with instructional programs offered at those levels.

The remainder of this chapter will discuss each of these important department head responsibilities and will suggest ways in which administrators can guide their chairmen's efforts to carry them out.

SERVING AS
DEPARTMENTAL CURRICULUM CONSULTANT

A good department head is a valuable resource person for the teachers in his department. He is a resident curriculum consultant, a teacher-leader who is knowledgeable about his subject and about the latest methods of teaching it effectively.

This is the ideal. Can it be realized? The answer is yes—to the extent that a district and an individual chairman are willing and able to dedicate their resources to the effort.

Each school district must bear a share of the responsibility for achieving the goal. Districts must be willing to provide department heads with released time so that they can keep abreast of developments in their fields. A department head who carries a full teaching load is in no better position to keep up in his field than are the other teachers in his department. In addition, districts must provide chairmen with the necessary curriculum resources. Resource centers must be developed and maintained in each departmental office or in each chairman's own classroom, if no office space is available. Each resource center must be stocked with professional publications in the department's subject area, including periodicals and reference books. It should also house appropriate instructional materials such as records, tapes, filmstrips, slides, and models. And finally, districts must be ready to underwrite the cost of sending chairmen to attend conferences or to inspect promising instructional programs in schools located in other parts of the state or even other parts of the nation. Administrators who have undertaken such travel themselves can attest to the broadening, educational value of the experience; they must see the worth of providing similar opportunities for their key teachers and subject area specialists: their department heads.

Department heads must match their district's support of curriculum development with their own efforts. Administrators must supervise their chairmen closely to see that they effectively utilize the time and resources made available to them by their districts. This means, first of all, that each chairman must familiarize himself with the contents of the material purchased for his departmental resource center. Then he must see that the most useful information which he finds in this material is made available to his teachers. The effective school department head accomplishes this in several ways:

1. He clips articles from professional journals and similar sources for inclusion in resource files which are readily accessible to every teacher in the department. These files should contain at least one folder for every unit taught in the classes in that department. Into these folders go specific tips concerning ways in which the unit might be presented to classes, helpful background or interpretative articles, and like material. Administrators should require their chairmen to establish and maintain such files and to circulate periodically an up-to-date list of their contents. Folders like these are extremely useful for curriculum committees and for both new and experienced teachers who are preparing to present a unit of study.

2. He duplicates and circulates within his department articles which are of particular importance or which have broad application. Sometimes this kind of material may be presented in its entirety, but a chairman will save his teachers' time and insure more careful reading of the information which he is distributing if he will summarize or even outline the article. As a matter of course, administrators should require their chairmen to give them copies of all such material which is circulated. This will give administrators an indication of how active

their department heads are in serving as resource consultants for their colleagues. It will also help administrators to keep themselves informed about the latest and most important developments in the different subject fields taught in their schools.

Department heads should also be directed to disseminate in much the same way the information which they or their teachers receive while attending professional conferences and institutes.

PLANNING FOR CONFERENCE PARTICIPATION

Making efficient use of the resources offered by a conference requires careful planning on the part of the chairman who is authorized to attend. Without this advance preparation, he is apt to find himself sitting in on general and specialized section meetings in a fairly haphazard fashion, and he may well discover too late that he has missed some particularly useful discussions. Advance planning can help the chairman to avoid such wasteful and inefficient practices. Indeed, evidence of such advance preparation should be required by administrators before granting approval to a chairman to attend any professional meeting, especially when the chairman has asked his district to help underwrite the cost of his participation in the conference.

The effective school department head begins his preparation for attending a conference by carefully measuring the offerings listed on the program against the needs of his department. On the basis of such an examination, he prepares an institute program for himself, by scheduling himself for those section meetings in which the material to be presented will be most valuable to his own department. If it appears that there might be more such meetings than he personally will be able to attend, or if some of the sessions will deal with very specialized topics which could be most helpful to a particular teacher or two in his department, the chairman should explore the possibility of bringing a team of instructors from his department to accompany him at the conference. Each team member could then be assigned an individual program of section meetings to attend, reflecting departmental needs and his own particular needs as well. Thus, for example, the chairman might attend all of the general sessions and those committee meetings which deal with broad trends in his subject field or with leadership problems and techniques. At the same time, the other members of his department's delegation should be sitting in on specialized discussions of methods or materials to be used in particular classroom situations.

At the conclusion of the conference, each participant should be directed to prepare a summary of the information which was made available to him in his particular meetings. Administrators might establish the following distribution schedule for these reports:

1. A copy to be kept on file in the appropriate district office. This provides a measure of the worth of this particular conference and also of each delegate's level of partipation in it. Such information is valuable to district curriculum directors; it can also be helpful to district administrators who have to determine which conferences are worthwhile enough to merit continued underwriting of delegate expenses in future years.

2. A copy to be kept in each school principal's office. Again, this helps administrators at the local school level to keep current on developments in each subject area represented in their school's curricula. In addition, it can be useful in determining which delegates should or should not be selected to attend future conferences—which might include the department head himself.

3. Copies to be furnished to each chairman in that subject field in other schools in the district.

4. Sufficient copies to be circulated among the members of the department whose delegates attended the conference. These reports might well stimulate fruitful discussion of curriculum methods and materials at the next department meeting.

5.   A copy to be retained in the resource files established in the department office.

We have seen why the department head is the logical person to serve as the primary resource consultant for the teachers in his department. His very accessibility makes him the person to whom they will most likely turn for guidance. A district may wish to provide additional support in the task of helping teachers to keep apprised of the lastest developments in their fields by establishing a central curriculum library at the district level, staffed with full-time general consultants. But, to quote a study of outstanding English departments conducted by the National Council of Teachers of English: "The effectiveness of this arrangement...can be judged only by the use teachers make of the library. Observation by the staff of the National Study Committee suggests that the greater the distance between English classroom and resource center, the less the resources are used."[4]

Thus, the responsibility falls mainly to the department head. If he receives adequate support and direction, an effective school department head can accomplish a great deal to keep his department's curriculum development program active and up-to-date.

IMPROVING COMMUNICATION WITHIN THE DEPARTMENT

As stated earlier, the second major contribution which a department head can make toward stimulating curriculum development in his department is to provide opportunities for his teachers to exchange ideas based on their own classroom experiences. There is a crucial need for effective department head leadership in providing such opportunities. Typically, the instructor in a large, modern school experiences a sense of some isolation from his colleagues. He is closeted away in his room during much of the day, totally absorbed in the process of teaching, whose highly complex intellectual, social, and psychological interactions between student and instructor place enormous demands on his time and energy. When he does have an opportunity to emerge from his room, the teacher will usually still find himself involved in school duties: supervising the campus, chaperoning activities, attending meetings which sometimes allow very little active participation on his own part, and, of course, grading papers and preparing for the next day's classes. As a result, the instructor has little opportunity to share ideas and experiences with his colleagues in the department.

Finding ways to combat this teacher isolation is a major challenge confronting every department head; the results of his effort have critical implications for curriculum development in his subject field. Unless his teachers are in the habit of communicating frequently and effectively with each other concerning their teaching, they will have little sense of common purpose underlying their efforts. Without this, a department really has no identity and no curriculum; it becomes merely a loose confederation of individuals proceeding more or less independently in their own rooms.

There are several ways in which an administrator can guide the department head's efforts to improve communications within his department and to provide opportunities for teachers to exchange ideas and experiences growing out of their classroom work.

Initially, administrators should point out the necessity for each chairman to set and maintain an open, positive, and encouraging tone in his professional relationships with his teachers. The department head must understand that as "prime minister" of the group, he establishes the climate among his teachers. If he is dictatorial, moody, cynical, or aloof, he will not encourage his colleagues to share their ideas and experiences with him. Without the establishment of this essential pattern of professional communication, he cannot expect his teachers to develop other than casual and infrequent professional contacts with each other. By contrast, the effective school department head makes himself readily available to his colleagues, and the door to his office or classroom will be open long before and after the hours of the regular school day. Unless he is confronted by an urgent deadline, he will always be ready to set his own work aside and talk with his staff. Moreover, he will not be merely a passive, although receptive, listener; he will also seek out his colleagues at every opportunity to engage them in positive, professional discussions concerning the department's instructional programs.

In addition, the department head can create situations in which the teachers in his department are removed from their separate rooms and placed in more continuous contact with each other. If his district has a policy of encouraging its faculty to visit other schools or other districts, the department head can arrange for his teachers to make these visits in teams of two or three and to report their observations to the rest of the staff at an early department meeting. If his school has facilities which permit team teaching to be carried on, the chairman can schedule his teachers to work together as dual or team instructors in large classes.

He may also create differentiated teaching teams, perhaps led by an outstanding senior member of the department who is supported by one or two younger teachers and a para-professional aide. The members of such a team should have differentiated assignments, reflecting the varied degrees of skill and experience which each could contribute to the united effort. Policies and situations such as these will encourage teachers to engage in continuous exchanges of ideas and information with each other.

In schools which do not have the resources or facilities necessary for faculty visitations or regularly-scheduled teaching teams, a department head can still work to improve communications within his department. Administrators might recommend to their chairman something like the following activity as one means of accomplishing this objective:

At the beginning of one school year, the teachers in the author's department were asked to fill out two sheets of paper. On one, they listed the units which they most enjoy teaching during the school year. On the other, they named the units which they have the least enthusiasm for teaching, either because they have covered them too often or because the concepts or techniques involved are difficult for them to present effectively. At a subsequent department meeting, copies of the two sheets were circulated and discussed. As might be expected, many teachers discovered that the material which they liked least was someone else's favorite. When this occurred, the instructors involved combined or exchanged their classes when the time came to present the particular unit in the class of the one who did not enjoy doing it. The discussions between teachers which were required to facilitate these short-term class groupings or exchanges did a great deal to help keep the lines of communication open within the department.

In a number of instances, where classes couldn't be combined or exchanged, the author took over one teacher's classes for a few days in order to free him to present a unit in another instructor's room. In these cases, the other teacher was able to observe and assist the visiting "specialist." This kind of experience tends to spark departmental interest in developing team teaching on a more regular basis and leads to increased communication and cooperation among the staff.

One of the most readily available forums for the exchange of ideas concerning teaching methods and materials within a department is, of course, the regular department meeting. Some guidelines for planning worthwhile department meetings in which these and other topics of importance can be discussed effectively will be presented in the next chapter.

SELECTING INSTRUCTIONAL MATERIALS

If teachers are to do effective work in their classrooms, they must have a voice in selecting the materials with which they teach. Therefore, after a department has developed instructional programs which incorporate the latest ideas and techniques, the chairman must be directed to involve his staff in the process of evaluating and selecting the books and other resources which they will use to implement that program. Administrators may suggest the following as ways in which this can be done easily and efficiently:

1. A chairman simply circulates catalogues within his department (if it is a large one), or he devotes part of a regular or special staff meeting to the examination of such catalogues. In either case, teachers in the department are asked to indicate the items which they want to have purchased and made available for their use. They are also asked to specify just how the desired material will help them to meet the department's established educational objectives and how the items relate to books or other instructional resources which are already a part of the department's resources. Information of

this type helps to insure that materials are not bought without good reason and that items which are purchased will receive maximum usage.

2.   An alternative procedure reverses the sequence just described. Starting with the department's specified objectives and with its existing instructional resources, the chairman and his colleagues work together to identify gaps and weaknesses in the materials already available to the department. These inadequacies might take the form of obsolete or insufficient books, slides, etc., required for effective teaching of a particular subject which is important in achieving the department's educational goals. With these needs clearly determined, it then becomes the chairman's responsibility to find the best materials that can be obtained to meet the department's requirements.

These same processes of screening and selecting materials may, of course, be delegated to grade level or subject area coordinators or committees. In either case, however, it remains the duty of the effective school department head to see that the evaluation and selection processes established within the school are efficiently carried out.

IMPROVING ARTICULATION WITH SCHOOLS AND COLLEGES

Successfully articulating the curricula of a secondary school with the programs of the elementary schools below and the colleges above poses an extremely challenging and time-consuming task for administrators and their staffs. But the links between the three levels of instruction must be established if the school is to offer its students worthwhile programs of instruction. Such programs build logically on the preparation accomplished in the lower school, but do not repeat it. They also prepare the school's graduates for a smooth transition into the more advanced studies offered in colleges and universities.

The process of articulation must eventually involve the entire staff of a school because of its implications for every department in that school. However, administrators can utilize their department heads to accomplish much of the preliminary work in each subject area. This will insure that when the teachers in each department begin to discuss their goals and procedures with elementary school or college staffs, they will be in a position to use their time and efforts most efficently.

Administrators should draw up a logical, sequential plan of action for their chairmen to follow in undertaking the initial work of articulation. Such a plan might involve these three phases:

1. Visitations by department heads,
2. Inter-school meetings,
3. Follow-up communication.

The effective school department head begins the process of articulation by visiting the elementary schools and colleges concerned, to familiarize himself with their programs and materials. While there, he makes a point of obtaining sample texts, placement tests, reading lists, and similar items for his teachers to examine. He also asks to sit in on several classes in his subject area, to study at first-hand the techniques used at both levels. During his visits to elementary schools, he reports to the teachers there on the kinds of successes and failures which their graduates typically experience when entering the high school. And while visiting each college, he familiarizes himself with the achievement records of his own school's graduates who have entered that institution.

While he is gathering this information for his school and department, the chairman also takes this opportunity to describe his own department's programs to the elementary and college teachers with whom he meets. The author has found that administrators and instructors on both of these levels welcome this information, particularly if it is accompanied by departmental book lists, courses of study, and sample assignment sheets. He has discovered that elementary school people too often structure their courses on the basis of incorrect assumptions about the high school's curricula; similarly, college programs frequently duplicate a great deal of what the high school of today is already teaching. Elementary and college teachers sometimes have little idea of what actually takes place in the high school classroom, and so the department head who provides insights here is rendering an invaluable service to all levels of education.

Once the initial visitations to the elementary schools and colleges have taken place, the chairman is ready to involve all of his teachers in the task of improving articulation of their instructional programs. Administrators might direct their chairmen to begin by sharing the materials and experiences which they gained on the visitations. Department heads should then be directed to work with their staffs to identify problem areas, where articulation appears to be weak, at either the beginning or end of the high school program. Lists of these possible areas of concern should then be sent to the elementary schools and colleges concerned, and meetings should be scheduled with the appropriate faculties of those institutions.

These conferences might assume various formats. Perhaps ideally, the entire staff of each high school department visits the elementary schools which furnish its entering students, to discuss the problems of articulation which had been identified earlier and also to study the elementary school situation at first hand. A follow-up meeting is then held at the high school, to work out any problems still remaining from the first sessions and also to give the elementary teachers a chance to inspect the high school's facilities and materials. This process is then repeated for each of the colleges to which large numbers of the high school's graduates apply for admission.

If this procedure seems too time-consuming for the three faculties involved, the chairman might be directed to schedule those of his teachers who generally teach first year classes to meet with elementary teachers and those who most often teach junior and senior classes to meet with the college representatives. These two groups then report to each other at a later department meeting, where recommendations designed to improve articulation will be discussed and acted upon by the total group.

Once the process of articulation improvement is thus begun, the effective school department head sees that it is continued in the future. This involves additional follow-up visits on his part, to keep up on any new developments which have changed elementary school or college programs. In addition, he invites representatives from the elementary school and college staffs to meet periodically with his own department (either as a whole or in committee), to continue their discussions of the problems of articulation. He also sees that exchanges of courses of study, book lists, and assignment sheets continue, at least on an annual basis.

A CHECK LIST FOR ADMINISTRATORS

This chapter has proposed a step-by-step program of action designed to develop school department heads who are effective leaders in curriculum development. We have examined the ways in which administrators can guide their chairmen in the work of defining specific educational goals and helping teachers to achieve those goals through writing and implementing up-to-date, articulated instructional programs. The following check list summarizes the essential steps involved in this process. It can be used to review each department head's present effectiveness as a leader in curriculum development and to pinpoint existing needs for additional administrative direction.

		Yes	No
1.	Has the department defined the goals of its instructional program?	——	——
2.	Are these objectives stated as much as possible in terms of specific, measurable student performance?	——	——
3.	Does the chairman maintain an efficient and helpful curriculum resource center for his staff?	——	——
4.	Does the chairman regularly bring to the attention of his teachers materials which report the latest developments in curriculum philosophy, methods, and materials in their subject area?	——	——
5.	When the chairman requests authorization to attend a professional conference, does he present for administrative review his plans for making the most effective use of the resources offered at the conference?	——	——
6.	After attending conferences and institutes, does the chairman regularly make worthwhile reports to the school and district?	——	——
7.	Does the chairman encourage his teachers to exchange ideas concerning curriculum		

Yes No

and instruction with him and with each other? — —

8. Does the department have a specific program for stimulating cooperative teaching activities among its members? — —

9. Does the chairman effectively involve his staff in selecting books and other curriculum materials? — —

10. Has the chairman visited appropriate elementary schools and colleges within the past five years, to improve communication and articulation? — —

11. Does the department regularly meet or exchange information and materials with elementary schools and colleges? — —

5

Making the Department Head an Effective Executive Manager

A conscientious department head may sometimes feel that he wears too many hats in his position: his duties are so varied that it becomes difficult for a single individual to cope with them all. Not only should a chairman be a master teacher, a subject matter expert, and the curricular and instructional leader of his department, but he must also be an efficient departmental administrator, providing a host of executive and managerial services for his colleagues.

More than one chairman who was interviewed by the author during the course of his project admitted that he was unable to meet all of these responsibilities. In order to survive, these individuals had decided to concentrate their efforts toward meeting certain obligations as effectively as possible, while allowing others to somehow "muddle through." In some cases, these department heads chose to work hardest on improving the curriculum and the quality of instruction in their departments, feeling (quite rightly, in the author's opinion) that these were their most important responsibilities. Others had given up trying to provide effective classroom supervision and had simply become efficient but expensive clerks for their departments, busying themselves with the requisitions, surveys, and reports which piled up on their desks each day.

Neither of these compromises can be acceptable to school administrators who wish to see their faculties led by effective department heads. Such administrators recognize that their chairmen need the kind of guidance which will help them to define their responsibilities in the area of departmental administration and will then help them to develop the kinds of skills necessary to meet those responsibilities efficiently.

What are the most important executive-managerial functions of the school department head? This chapter will examine the role of the chairman in providing the following services for his department:

1. Serving as spokesman for his subject area in meetings with school and community groups of various kinds,

2. Planning and chairing departmental, grade level, and special area meetings,

3. Developing and administering the departmental budget,

4. Handling the paper work essential to any office operation.

Administrators will find in this review many practical suggestions for use in a training program for both new and experienced department chairmen. These ideas are drawn from the experiences of the many department heads interviewed by the author during his study who have found the way to wear all of their hats comfortably—and effectively.

SERVING AS DEPARTMENT SPOKESMAN

Department heads are frequently called upon to provide liaison between their colleagues and groups of administrators, teachers, or citizens in the community. However time-consuming such assignments may seem to be, the effective school department head views them as opportunities to render an important service for his department and his school. Whenever he speaks for his teachers or his program, he can provide useful information—and win valuable support. Thus, a conscientious, articulate chairman is an invaluable resource specialist and public relations agent for school administrators on all levels.

As spokesman for his department, a chairman may find himself asked to explain new developments in his subject area to groups of parents at a PTA meeting. Perhaps he will be questioned by visiting administrators, teachers, or parents regarding new courses, instructional practices, or departmental policies, such as those established for grading or tracking students. He will sometimes be interviewed by the school or community press or be asked to write summaries of his department's programs for the school's student handbook or counselors' guide. In any of these situations, the department head may find himself explaining, advocating, or even occasionally defending.

Much depends on the effectiveness of the chairman's presentations on behalf of his department. If he has not prepared himself thoroughly about the details of his subject, or if he does not utilize his skill as a master teacher to present his information convincingly, he may lose an important opportunity to inform and to win support. Officials who might otherwise have approved a course of action instead will oppose it. Interested students will be turned away from a department's program where they might have been attracted to it. A chance to develop better public relations will be bungled. The department head must understand that important consequences can develop from his performance as spokesman for his subject or department.

Administrators who wish their chairman to realize the importance of this responsibility should review with their chairman the possible benefits to department and school offered by speaking assignments. Further, they should stress the rules of effective communication when guiding their chairmen in the task of planning and making such presentations:

1. **Be prepared** The department head should know his material thoroughly. If necessary, he should consult with other members of his department to obtain needed information. On occasion, he might ask one or more of his teachers (particularly those working in highly specialized subjects) to accompany him on speaking engagements, to serve as resource persons. In addition, the chairman should know his audience's needs, expectations, and level of familiarity with his subject matter.

2.   **Be brief** This, of course, is the cardinal rule for all speakers. Unless the chairman is an accomplished speaker or writer, he would be wise to limit his presentation to not more than fifteen minutes or a few pages in length.

3.   **Be efficient** Only an untrained speaker tries to cover every conceivable aspect of his subject; there is truth in the old saying that the person who tries to exhaust his topic only exhausts his audience. Instead, efficient communication requires that the spokesman understand and follow a particular process. This process has three distinct stages: presentation, interaction, and reinforcement. During the presentation stage, information is transmitted. But real communication occurs only after this information has been assimilated by the audience. Thus, the effective spokesman provides an opportunity for his listeners to do something with what they have heard: to question him or to discuss the information among themselves. In this interactive phase, the audience is playing an active role in the communication process by making the material which it has just heard a part of its own thinking. And finally, the effective chairman reinforces his major points at the conclusion of his presentation by an oral or written summary. A written outline is a particularly efficient tool by which to achieve reinforcement; distributing such at the conclusion of an oral presentation helps to fix the speaker's information in the audience's minds and also provides a useful reference in any future review of his topic.

What has been discussed here concerning the process and procedures involved in effective communication is, of course, familiar to every master teacher. If the department head is the outstanding instructor that he should be, he will probably use these techniques in his own classroom. Administrators need only remind him to follow the same process and use the same skills when he serves as spokesman for his subject or his department.

PLANNING AND CONDUCTING
WORTHWHILE DEPARTMENT MEETINGS

The task of planning and presiding over worthwhile meetings ranks high on any list of department head responsibilities. It is a fact of academic life that the school year is marked by cycles of meetings: meetings to open school, department and faculty gatherings periodically throughout the year, and even meetings to close school. These sessions eat into the all-too-limited time available to teachers for their own classroom responsibilities, and if they do not see themselves gaining something of value, they will resent being asked to attend "meetings for the sake of meetings."

Administrators therefore need to devote considerable effort to the task of helping their chairmen improve the quality of the meetings which they plan and conduct within their departments. They must guide their chairmen to think beyond sessions in which announcements are read to passive groups of silent teachers who know full well that such material could have been brought to their attention far more efficiently through departmental memoranda. When busy teachers are called together for nothing more interesting and important than that, their morale and their teaching effectiveness are bound to suffer.

Administrators might begin the process of guiding their chairman in this area by asking them a simple but fundamental question: what is the value of holding department meetings at all? When the department head has thought through a clear and logical answer to this question, he will have developed a useful guideline for evaluating his plans for such meetings in the future.

In the author's opinion, department meetings can accomplish a number of important and desirable objectives. For one, such sessions can strengthen a group's sense of common identity and purpose. As the individual teachers who make up a department gather from time to time, they begin to lose that sense of isolation and drift which affects teachers who spend too much time in their separate classrooms, cut off from professional interaction with each other. In addition, drawing individuals together from time to time improves communication within the department. This can take place at the meeting itself, of course, if the chairman is skillful enough to stimulate and guide it. Such communication can also begin at the meeting and then continue in small group discussions for days and weeks afterward, if the agenda prepared by the chairmen is sufficiently interesting to the teachers involved. And finally, the collected faculty of a department represents an extremely useful gathering of wisdom and experience; out of its interactions can come decisions of great value for improving a department's instructional programs.

How can a department head plan and conduct meetings which will help to draw his teachers together into a unified group, encourage better communication among them, and also make the best use of their united talents for the benefit of the department's work? Administrators might stress some of the following points as they work with their chairmen.

To a large degree, the success or failure of any meeting will depend on the care which a chairman takes in selecting the agenda. A department head who wishes to conduct worthwhile meetings will include in that agenda only items which have interest and value for the group and which can be considered in no better way than at a meeting of the total group. Anything which is trivial in nature or which could be handled as well by memos from the chairman should be rigorously excluded from the program. A chairman cannot expect good results from his meetings if he clutters them with items which he is too lazy or too inefficient to take care of in a more appropriate way.

There are other factors to be weighed carefully in planning for good department meetings. A chairman should be sensitive to the kinds of demands which are being made on his teachers at any given time. Thus, a meeting set for the same day that term tests are to be given or report cards are to be filled out will probably be a dull affair for most teachers and should be rescheduled for a better time if this can be done. The chairman should also take into account the prevailing mood of his staff, reflecting anything from the time of year to trends in salary negotiations or even the fortunes of the school's football team, when he plans for his meetings.

Perhaps most importantly, however, the effective school department head considers the interests and needs of his teachers and plans his meetings accordingly. One technique which the author has found useful in learning about the interests and needs of his own colleagues is the periodic, open-ended questionnaire. From time to time, the author has asked his teachers the following questions:

1. What changes *within your classrooms* would be of most help to you this year? These might involve your teaching assignment, the room facilities as you find them, the books and other materials which are available, or whatever.

2. What changes would you like to see take place this year *in the department?* Please mention any policies, programs, or activities which in any way affect your individual work as a teacher in this department.

3. What changes would you like to have occur *within the school* or *within the district* to improve your position as a teacher and to make your work as enjoyable and successful as possible?

The responses from these questionnaires have provided many insights into the kinds of topics which the author should select for discussion at department meetings. These discussions have frequently led to decisions and actions which have been helpful to the morale and performance of members of the department, both individually and collectively.

Once a chairman has selected the material for his agenda, however, he must not think that he has completed all of the advance preparation required for a good, productive meeting. His next concern must be to find ways in which to involve his staff actively in the consideration of each item. One way to accomplish this is to ask particular teachers both to present appropriate items for the group's consideration and to lead the ensuing discussion. This tactic serves several worthwhile purposes: it helps stimulate greater participation and communication within the group, and it also encourages the expression of ideas which might never have occurred to the chairman. Indeed, for many reasons the effective school department head resists the temptation to use his department meetings as a stage on which to parade his personality and talents.

Finally, chairmen should also give careful thought to the kind of format which they wish to adopt for their meetings. The author recommends the following as a procedure which seems to encourage group achievement of the goals of unity, communication, and deliberation.

The first part of each meeting is generally informal in tone. Its purpose is to provide an opportunity for the department staff to make the transition from individuals into group. Refreshments are served during this time, and teachers in the department are invited to come to the meeting place as soon as convenient, to share conversation and a relaxing cup of coffee with each other. When the meeting actually begins, the first items on the agenda are generally brief and of a nature to draw forth casual comments from many of the assembled teachers. Subjects for consideration in this first part of each session often include follow-up comments on items discussed at a previous meeting or discussions of projected activities such as field trips, which might involve many members of the department.

Following this introductory period, the topics in the agenda become increasingly important and professionally challenging in tone and nature. There often are panel presentations by teachers involved in particular experiments whose outcome might affect the department's instructional programs. Guests are frequently invited from outside the school to examine those programs in terms of the needs of colleges or businesses which receive the school's graduates. Periodically, the entire department engages in a systematic, intensive self-examination, which might continue over a period of several months. In such moments, the intra-group communication is at its highest, and the talents and experiences of the entire staff are utilized to their fullest.

As one example of such an experience in self-analysis and self-direction for a department, the questions listed below were addressed by the author to his own teachers at a meeting early one year. As planned, the group then divided into interest committees to consider each of the three major groups of questions (personnel, programs, materials) separately. After a few minutes, however, it became apparent that every member of the department wanted to contribute his own ideas and experiences to the answering of every question. As a result, the department voted to use the entire list of fifteen questions as the major item for consideration in department meetings throughout the year, discussing two or three at each session. The author is convinced that the meetings held that year were among the most productive in his experience. These discussions contributed a great deal to strengthening the department's instructional programs and to shaping their future development.

It will be noted that the questions on this particular list relate most directly to the work of an English department. However, it would not be difficult for administrators or department heads to revise them so as to make them apply in any other subject area.

A. Personnel

1. Is there a proper balance of teaching strengths in the present staff of the department? Are we weighted too heavily with specialists in literature, at the expense of specialists in language and composition? What will be the future needs of the department in recruiting and employing new personnel? How can we pool our efforts to find and employ the kind of teachers that we want to have working as our colleagues?

2. What improvements are needed in the training, assignment, and evaluation of new teachers in the department? How can veteran teachers help in these tasks?

3. How should the department evaluate the effectiveness of teachers who have received tenure?

4. What improvements are needed in the executive direction of the department? Should there be grade level or subject coordinators? Should the position of department head be

rotated among members of the department? Should we consider splitting into two departments (required and elective classes), with separate chairmen for each?

5.   How can we create teams of teachers and para-professional aides to strengthen our instructional programs?

B.   Programs

1.   Are we doing a good enough job of teaching each part of the English tripod (language, literature, and composition)? How do we know? What improvements are needed, and how can we bring them about?

2.   Should there be major changes in the overall content of our courses? Should we restructure classes to focus on particular English skills or literary classifications (genre, theme) at particular levels?

3.   What new courses should the department plan to offer, and in what order of priority should they be introduced? Will these new courses create the need for new personnel, with skills not presently found among our staff?

4.   Is our present tracking or grouping policy satisfactory? Are we equally successful in teaching all of our present tracks? Should we experiment with other ways of grouping our students?

5.   How can we measure the value of any course? How can we better assess what has been gained by a student who has completed a particular subject?

C. Materials

1.   How can we set up a more systematic and ef-

fective way of evaluating the usefulness of our instructional resources (books, audio-visual materials, classroom supplies and equipment, etc.)?

2. What materials should be phased out of or into our programs, and in what order of priority should this be done?

3. Should any changes be made in the physical structure of our classrooms?

4. How can we make better instructional use of non-classroom areas throughout the school, such as courtyards and lawns?

5. What systematic use can we make of the richly varied educational resources available to us through our proximity to San Francisco?

In addition to planning and conducting meetings of a total department such as described above, the effective school department head must also expect to participate in a variety of other, more specialized meetings.

Some of these may take place within his own school, involving committees of teachers drawn from his department. When such groups meet by grade level or subject area to discuss book evaluations and adoptions, general policies or particular practices, the department head should be present. It is often desirable that he ask someone else to chair these sessions and that he attend merely to listen to the proceedings and to participate as requested. Regardless of the extent of his active participation in such meetings, however, the chairman accomplishes several desirable objectives simply by being present. To begin with, his presence lends a sense of importance to the work at hand; a meeting which is attended by the leader of a group generally assumes greater significance in the eyes of the group. In addition, visiting these committee sessions keeps the department head better informed about the thinking of his staff. And finally, as he watches a group at work, the chairman is able to evaluate each member's contributions; this insight will prove useful in the future when the chairman is asked to make recommendations for assignments, tenure, and promotion.

A department head is frequently asked to conduct or attend other meetings. These may involve other chairmen from his school who serve as a principal's advisory cabinet, or other department heads in his subject area from throughout a district who serve on a superintendent's district council. In either case, the department head must be present, to keep himself informed on matters which may affect his own staff and to make appropriate contributions from his own ideas and experience. Beyond this, a chairman can increase the effectiveness of his participation in meetings at these levels if he will involve his teachers in the proceedings, as much as possible. He can do this by posting the agendas of these meetings in advance, thereby encouraging his colleagues to express their own views on matters to be decided at the meetings. Moreover, he can circulate the minutes of these meetings to the teachers in his department, to inform them about any actions which were taken.

These procedures strengthen the morale of a department because they make the teachers feel that they are truly important parts of the school and district. They also make the department head a more effective and democratic leader. Such a chairman properly represents his subject field and his colleagues and draws upon the collective wisdom of the entire group to help him make important decisions.

ADMINISTERING THE DEPARTMENTAL BUDGET

To a very real degree, a department's budget outlines the department's educational objectives and establishes the limits of its instructional programs.

This significant fact is gaining increased recognition, particularly in districts which adopt program planning and budgeting systems. As a consequence, school administrators must give their chairmen special training, to guide them in developing departmental budgets which will move their instructional programs forward in logical, systematic, and continuous fashion. There are various ways in which this can be accomplished; the key element in all is that the effective school department head plans in advance to meet specific objectives, within guidelines set by the district and school.

A chairman must exercise careful judgment when he begins to

develop his department's budget. He knows that good teachers can accomplish much with quite limited resources, but he also realizes that creativity and ingenuity cannot be expected to substitute indefinitely for adequate funding. A department requires money in order to maintain its existing programs, and additional funds will normally be required to finance major improvements in those programs. It thus becomes the chairman's task, under administrative direction, to prepare a budget which will make it possible for a department to continue to function during the coming year. It must also provide for innovations to be introduced, to a degree that is realistic in view of the requirements of the department's objectives and the availability of financial resources in the school and district.

In allocating funds between these two objectives, the effective school department head takes into account the requirements of his entire department. This means that he confers with his entire staff, usually meeting with them in grade level or subject area committees. In these conferences, each teacher has an opportunity to outline his requirements for the coming year in terms of supplies, equipment, facilities, personnel, or other special categories. It is helpful for the development of a truly efficient budget if these needs are differentiated into at least three distinct categories:

1. Items which are essential to maintain effective existing programs of instruction in each classroom for another year. The emphasis here is generally upon replacement costs rather than acquisition costs.

2. Items which are required to implement programs essential to achieving new, intermediate-range goals previously established within the department.

3. Items which will permit all segments of the department to undertake quite far-reaching experiments in educational innovation. These items constitute a kind of "dream" budget for the department.

The compilation of lists such as these enables a department head to develop a budget designed to accomplish very specific educational objectives. Under administrative guidance, the chairman designates those areas which will continue to function at approximately the same level for another year. He also determines where additional funds should be allocated, to support instructional strategies designed to achieve significant new objectives. His decisions must, of course, have the consent and support of the teachers in his department.

When every department in a school establishes such priorities and prepares budgets accordingly, it becomes easy for their chairmen to work closely with the building principal to develop a budget for the school which provides for maximum improvement in the school's total instructional program. This improvement should be projected into the future over a span of years, with specific goals established for each department in each of those years. These procedures insure that good, well-established programs in each department will continue to be maintained. They also insure that major improvements will be introduced into each subject area in a logical sequence, within the limits of the district's ability to provide funds to support them.

Once his budget has been established, the department head has the responsibility of seeing that it is administered fairly and efficiently. This means that his purchase requisitions must implement the decisions reached by the department and the school when the budget was developed; any deviations should have both departmental and administrative sanction. In addition, the chairman needs to keep accurate records of his expenditures, to make certain that he does not exceed the limits or intentions of the budget. The author has found that the simple ledger illustrated below is sufficient for keeping his own departmental records. A form such as this makes it possible to monitor the level of expenditures for each program in the department. It also provides

_____ DEPARTMENT EXPENDITURES

School Year ____

Program	Date Ordered	Date Rec'd	Items	Cost	Amount Spent to Date on Program	Total Spent to Date	Balance to Date

running totals for all expenditures and up-to-date balances, so that the department's financial situation can quickly be assessed at any time.

Obviously, more sophisticated procedures and forms may be developed for use by department heads in all subject fields, particularly in districts which have committed themselves to program planning and budgeting systems. The form illustrated above, however, may serve the present needs of many school administrators throughout the country whose chairmen require guidance in developing techniques which will enable them to manage their budgets effectively.

MANAGING DEPARTMENTAL OFFICE DUTIES

A final important responsibility of the department head, in his role as departmental manager, is to handle the myriad routine details connected with the day-to-day operations of his department. Even the most conscientious chairman sometimes feels himself bogged down in these "nuts and bolts" chores, and the frustration which he experiences as a result can seriously impair the effectiveness of his overall leadership in his department.

What are these routine—but important—duties which can prove so time-consuming? During a given day, a chairman finds himself doing any or all of the following:

1. Preparing departmental reports and surveys,
2. Receiving, distributing, and frequently answering departmental correspondence,
3. Conferring with sales representatives or district business personnel regarding equipment, supplies, books, etc.,
4. Requisitioning equipment and supplies for the department,
5. Requisitioning books and other instructional materials for the department.
6. Supervising equipment inventory and repair within the department.

Administrators who perform similar or related duties on their own levels in a school or district know full well how this "paper work" routine can chain them to their desks. If they want their chairmen to have time to work with their teachers, for the improvement of departmental instructional programs, principals and other administrators will need to find ways of helping their chairmen cope with these duties. The author suggests the following three courses of action as possible starting points for administrative consideration.

In a number of schools which the author visited while conducting his study of the department head position, administrators had begun to experiment with establishing co-chairman positions in some departments, particularly in those with large numbers of teachers. In such cases, one chairman assumes responsibility for supervising curriculum and instruction in the department, while the other takes charge of all business and related responsibilities.

Each chairman may have a released period daily during which to perform these duties. In most schools, however, only the "instructional" chairman is provided with released time. The "office" chairman receives extra pay, to compensate for the time which he spends after the regular school day, handling the business affairs of the department. This division of responsibilities is modeled on that found in schools which have established the position of assistant principal in charge of business operations, in order to free the principal to play a more active role in curriculum development and instructional supervision within the school.

Other districts have preferred to retain single department head positions, in order to retain unity of leadership within the department, but have employed clerks or teacher aides to handle routine departmental business. The benefits to be derived from providing this kind of assistance for department heads seem so obvious that the author has included this in Part Two of this book as a major recommendation for improving department head performance. One benefit to be gained from increased allocation of such para-professional assistance is more efficient use of expensive teacher time. Released time for department heads, who are most often experienced teachers at the top of their district salary schedules, is extremely expensive—averaging up to $3000 per period annually. To permit this time to be devoted to essentially clerical work seems to the author a most unsound practice, from both economic and educational standpoints. Instead, with even part-time secretarial help to free him from these routine chores, the chairman is able to concentrate his efforts in the areas where he should be most effective and most valuable to his school and district: in curriculum and instruction. Indeed, if a department head's talents did not lie mainly in these areas, one might question the appropriateness of retaining him in his position.

Administrators should also find ways in which to streamline and simplify the business operations of departments in their schools. A good place to begin this simplification is with the procedures which have been established for requisitioning supplies and equipment. Many chairmen interviewed by the author complained of the hours which they spend annually poring through supply and equipment catalogues, copying down the precise specifications for items which they intend to order. When one considers, for an example, that each year every science department head in a district may well be examining the same catalogues, often at the same time, in search of the same information, it seems obvious that a great deal of wasteful duplication of effort is occurring. As an alternative to this all-too-common practice, the author recommends that districts create standardized supply and equipment lists for each subject area, to be used in every school in the district. Such lists were recently prepared in the author's own district in California, and they have proved very helpful in simplifying every department head's managerial responsibilities.

The supply and equipment lists adopted in the San Mateo Union High School District were prepared in such a way that they reflect the best thinking of the entire district faculty. Initially, teachers and department heads in each subject area met in small groups, to consider the requirements of a particular kind of teaching station found in their discipline. Thus, for example, English teachers and department heads met in sub-committees to draw up lists of equipment needed for effective teaching in regular classrooms, team rooms, drama and speech classrooms, reading laboratories, departmental resource centers, and so forth. In each case, the committee involved was asked to envision an empty room and then to choose the kinds of equipment which should be provided for that room and the priorities to be assigned for bringing in each particular item. Agreement was also reached on desirable specifications for the equipment selected. As might be imagined, these initial decisions were not always arrived at easily. But in the sometimes heated discussions which took place in each teacher group, a great deal of useful information concerning instructional methods and materials was exchanged. These teacher-constructed lists later received administrative review and approval.

The supply and equipment lists now standardized by subject and teaching station in the author's district have served a number of worthwhile purposes. Naturally, they provide quick references for teachers in every department as they request materials which will bring their individual rooms up to optimum standards. This has been particularly useful to teachers and department heads selected to staff a new school, where large quantities of material must be ordered at one time. In addition, the lists simplify the department head's responsibilities in taking inventory of materials in his department and in ordering replacements or additions. Each list provides the kind of specific information about particular items which once took department heads hours to find; with these lists, requisitions can be prepared by the chairman or his assistant in a matter of minutes. And finally, the lists have proved easy to keep up-to-date. They are reviewed annually by district councils of department heads in each subject area, and necessary or desirable changes (often recommended by the district's business services staff) are quickly made.

Examples of the San Mateo Union High School District's supply and equipment lists appear on the following pages. It will be noted that the supply list given here has been prepared in the form of a purchase requisition; with this form at hand, a chairman need only jot down the quantity and the total cost of the items which he wishes to have purchased for his classrooms. This illustrates the kind of simplification of business responsibilities which a district can effect in order to save valuable department head time. Such a saving makes it possible for chairmen to involve themselves more fully in development of curriculum and improvement of instruction.

SAN MATEO UNION HIGH SCHOOL DISTRICT

School

Department

Subject

MATERIAL REQUISITION

CHEMICALS

Page 2 of 8

Requisition No. _____

Date _____

Account No. 13.0291-8120

PROJECT

ITEM NO.	DESCRIPTION	EQUAL TO MFG'S or SUPPLIER'S PART/CAT. NO.	BRAND/NO. QUOTED	QUANTITY REQ'D.	UNIT (ea, lb, etc.)	ESTIM. UNIT PRICE	TOTAL PRICE	ITEM NO.
21	BROM. THYMOL - BLUE 5 Gr	Cenco 39572			bottle	$6.30		21
22	1-BUTANOL, REAGENT	Cenco 37220			pint	1.01		22
23	2-BUTANOL, REAGENT	Cenco 39376			pint	1.20		23
24	TEST-BUTANOL, REAGENT	Cenco 37224			pint	.75		24
25	CALCIUM CARBIDE TECH.	Cenco 37528			lb	3.00		25
26	CALCIUM CARBONATE (Marble Chips)	Cenco 37536			lb	.75		26
27	CALCIUM CHLORIDE ANHYDROUS, Gran. 12 mesh	JTB 1310-05			5 lb	3.55		27
28	CALCIUM HYDROXIDE, TECH, Pwd.	Cenco 37564			lb	.85		28
29	CALCIUM NITRATE, AR, Gran.	JT 1395-1			lb	1.80		29
30	CALCIUM OXIDE, N. F., Pwd.	JTB 1414			lb	.90		30
31	CARBON DIOXIDE-LECTURE BOTTLE- Contents: 0.5 lb	Cenco 13800			bottle	8.25		31
32	CARBON TETRACHLORIDE, TECH	Cenco 37612			gal	6.48		32
33	CHLORINE, LECTURE BOTTLE-Contents; 1 lb	Cenco 13802			bottle	5.00		33
34	CHROMIUM SULFATE, AR, Cryst.	Cenco 37662			lb	4.19		34
35	CITRIC ACID, AR, ACS, Cryst.	Cenco 37046			lb	1.56		35
36	COBALT (II) NITRATE, AR, ACS, Cryst.	Cenco 37672			lb	4.66		36
37	COBALT (II) NITRATE, AR, ACS, Cryst.	MCW 4544			lb	4.11		37
38	COPPER, WIRE, BASE B&S 22 Gauge	Cenco 89561			lb	2.45		38
39	COPPER, WIRE, BASE B&S 16 Gauge	Cenco 89561			lb	2.25		39
40	COPPER, SHEET ,20 Gauge 12" x 12"	Cenco 89095			sheet	3.50		40

Instructor _____   Dept. Head _____   Principal _____   Ass't Supt _____

DEPARTMENT   SOCIAL STUDIES   EQUIPMENT LIST FOR   CONTEMPORARY PROBLEMS

(subject)

66-67

Item No.	Prior-ity No.	Item	Quantity Authorized	On Hand	Description (size, essential features, etc.)	Suggested Brand and Model No.	Estimated Cost
							$
1	1	Desks, Student	30		Standard size; natural oak finish		
2	1	Table	1		72" x 30". Natural oak w/plastic top.	Beckley-Cardy	46.25
3	1	Chairs	6		Natural oak finish.	Beckley-Cardy	
4	1	Desk, Instructor's	1		54" x 30". Double pedestal, plastic top 1¼" top; automatic locking device; natural oak finish.	Challenger	94.00
5	1	Chair, Instructor's	1		20½" x 19" x 16". Swivel, with arms natural oak.	Peerless	37.80
6	3	Chair Cushion	1		17" x 18". Foam Rubber	Goodyear	5.45
7	2	Typewriter Table	1		Natural oak finish, w/ drawer, plastic top.	Beckley-Cardy	17.95
8	1	Bookcases	2		36" x 9" x 48". Natural oak.	Beckley-Cardy	37.50
9	2	Lectern	1		Natural oak, stand-up shelves.	Beckley-Cardy	
10	1	Book Rack	1		16½" x 8". Natural oak.	Beckley-Cardy	2.45
11	2	Dictionary Holder	1		21" x 12" x 5½" Revolving, natural oak.	Beckley-Cardy	13.50
12	3	Lectern Light Fixture	1			Beckley-Cardy	6.50
13	3	Phonograph Cart	1		With storage rack. (if possible)	Beckley-Cardy 819	38.00
14	3	Tape Compartment	1		(if possible)	Beckley-Cardy 85-7	9.95
15	1	File Cabinet	2		Legal size, 4-drawer, sandalwood (color), with lock.	D214CP-38	70.35
16	2	Stool	1		Swivel, adjustable height, sandalwood or natural oak, padded seat and back.		
17	2	Tape Recorder	1		Mike, earphones, foot control.	Revere T-2200	
18	2	Phonograph	1		Mike, earphones, oatmeal beige.	Newcomb ED-1610	86.50

A CHECK LIST FOR ADMINISTRATORS

The many and varied executive responsibilities of the school department head have been surveyed in this final chapter in Part One of this book. Specific steps were proposed by which administrators on all levels can help their chairmen to organize, simplify, and effectively meet these obligations. By using the following check list, administrators will be able to identify problem areas in which their department heads need additional guidance.

		Yes	No
1.	Within the past year, has each chairman discussed his department's programs with an audience outside of the department?	___	___
2.	Does each chairman recognize the importance of his role as departmental spokesman?	___	___
3.	Does each chairman know how to plan and deliver an effective discussion of his department's programs?	___	___
4.	Does each chairman have a clearly defined understanding of the value of department meetings?	___	___
5.	Is each chairman flexible in scheduling and holding his department meetings?	___	___
6.	Within the past few years, has each chairman polled his teachers concerning topics which they want discussed at their meetings?	___	___
7.	Does each chairman know how to construct an effective agenda for his meetings, in order to interest and actively involve his staff?	___	___
8.	Does every chairman regularly attend grade level or other special meetings and keep his department informed about what takes place there?	___	___
9.	Does each chairman involve his entire staff in the preparation of the departmental budget?	___	___
10.	Does each department budget provide for the support of existing worthwhile instructional programs?	___	___

Yes   No

11. Does each department budget provide for the support of new programs which will be introduced systematically over a period of years to meet specific, established departmental objectives?   ___   ___

12. Does each department head keep an adequate record of his department's expenditures?   ___   ___

13. Does each chairman handle his office duties effectively?   ___   ___

14. Would his performance be improved if he had para-professional assistance in meeting those obligations?   ___   ___

15. Is each chairman actively engaged in efforts designed to simplify and streamline his office responsibilities?   ___   ___

16. Has the district considered or adopted standardized supply and equipment lists for each subject area?   ___   ___

Part Two

IMPROVING THE POSITION
OF THE DEPARTMENT HEAD
IN A DISTRICT

6

Upgrading the Selection

and Training

of Department Heads

At the conclusion of his year-long study of the department head position for the San Mateo Union High School District in California, the author prepared a report on his findings. The key part of this document was a series of recommendations for improving the policies and practices governing the selection, training, operations, and evaluation of department heads in his district. These proposals were drawn from the author's extensive research in professional literature and from his conferences with superintendents, principals, department heads, and teachers in school districts ranging from San Diego, California, to Portland, Oregon.

In the introduction to his project report, the author set forth the following rationale for his recommendations:

"In light of the vital position of the department head in his school, the following recommendations are offered.

"They are not money-savers for this district; indeed, they will require that the district invest even more of its resources in support of its department head positions.

"They are not people-savers either; instead they will make stringent demands on personnel at all levels in this district.

"But they are designed to make the department headship truly a career, professional position for the best teachers in this district, a position which will enable them to exercise some of the instructional leadership traditionally reserved for administrative positions.

"If these recommendations are accepted and enacted into district policy, they will make of the department head position one which only the able can fill, from which the able will derive great personal and professional rewards, and through which the able will render invaluable service to the San Mateo Union High School District."[5]

In this and the following chapters, administrators will find a full discussion of the author's recommendations to his own district. Presented here are some of the most successful leadership policies followed in districts with national reputations for excellence. They are offered for review by superintendents and their staffs who are seeking ways in which to improve their school systems. The author believes that these recommendations can accomplish very major improvements in the performance of those who hold department head appointments. And this, he is convinced, will produce an immediate and marked improvement in the teaching carried on in every classroom under their direction.

Whatever the outcome of these recommendations, whether administrators choose to accept them totally or in part, the author believes that they can be an essential first step toward making any district's department head position a model of efficiency and effectiveness.

Any plan for improving the department head position in a district must certainly begin with an examination of the process by which chairmen are selected and trained for their work. It must be clear that a position can never be stronger than the capabilities of the person who fills it. Therefore, this chapter will assess the strengths and weaknesses of a number of procedures for choosing and preparing new department heads. Some of these procedures have been discussed in recent professional literature; others were observed by the author in the districts which he visited during his study of the department headship.

The quality of the initial choice from among candidates for a department head vacancy is critically important in determining the level of performance which a district may reasonably expect from that position. If the system in operation within a particular district permits incompetent individuals to be selected, then the district initially handicaps itself in any future efforts to achieve substantial improvement in department head performance. This limitation will apply regardless of the level of support which the district is willing and able to provide its chairmen.

How *should* department heads be chosen? What procedures offer a district the best chance of finding and appointing the most capable applicants?

In general, department heads are selected by one of three methods: by administrative appointment (either on the school or district level), by election from within the department concerned, or by some combination of these two.

APPOINTING CHAIRMEN VS. ELECTING CHAIRMEN

The most frequently used procedure is that of appointment by school and/or district administrators; this was the practice followed in 77 per cent of the schools covered in one survey. [6] This method of selection has a number of advantages—but also some drawbacks. [7]

1. Administrators have the broadest view of the needs of the total school program, so they should be allowed to select the person who best meets those needs.

2. Administrators must work with the department head and are responsible for the effectiveness of his performance, so they should make the selection. (Administrators will undoubtedly choose a man whom they respect and with whom they will be able to work successfully.)

3. Appointment tends to clearly centralize authority

and responsibility in a department. (The chairman who is chosen by this method will be viewed by his teachers as the designated surrogate of the school and district administrations. As a result, such a chairman's recommendations to his staff will be respected as carrying with them administrative sanction and support.)

4. Selection by administrative appointment allows for a department head to be designated with minimal encroachment on the time and efforts of teachers in the department. They are thus left free to devote their attention to their classroom responsibilities.

On the other hand, the process of choosing department heads solely by administrative appointment carries with it certain possible dangers:

1. The administrators who make the selection must rely on their subjective evaluation of the qualifications of the apointee. (This can increase the margin for error in the choice, even though the candicate selected might have to be confirmed by district level administrators.)

2. A department may resent having no voice in the selection of its own leadership. (This resentment could linger, weakening the new chairman's chances of working effectively with the group in the future.)

3. Personality conflicts of various kinds can develop in a department if popular or senior teachers are passed over in the selection. (These individuals might organize opposition cliques within the department; such dissension would limit the future effectiveness of the group and its new leader alike.)

School and district administrators who are sensitive to these potential drawbacks in a system where chairmen are appointed might consider the alternative of allowing chairmen to be elected by ballot from among their colleagues. But this method of selection also has both advantages and disadvantages that must be weighed:[7]

1. Departmental morale might be improved by involving teachers in the selection of their own leadership. (This sharing of responsibility would enhance the professional stature of any school's faculty.)

2. The person elected to serve as chairman will probably be one who can get along well with the other members of his department. (As a result, personality conflicts and internal dissension like those occurring when chairmen are appointed could be reduced or eliminated.)

3. The teacher in the department with proven leadership ability will probably be chosen to serve as chairman. (The teachers making the selection know each other well and can be expected to pick the most capable individual from among their own ranks.)

Again, however, there are serious objections raised against procedures which provide for leadership through ballot:

1. The person elected to serve as chairman might not have the approval and support of school and district administrators. (In such a situation, they would tend to delegate very little authority and responsibility to the department head, thus seriously reducing his effectiveness as a leader.)

2. Competition for the chairman's position within a department can weaken the staff's sense of professional unity and cooperation. (Such competition actually encourages personality conflicts and other forms of internal dissension in a department.)

3. Election can tend to diffuse authority and responsibility within a department and destroy the continuity of leadership essential to any group's forward movement. (It is not difficult to conceive

of situations where influential teachers play the role of "kingmakers" in a department, replacing their chairmen virtually at will. Such individuals feel little responsibility for supporting their chairman's policies.)

4. Contrary to expectations, a department could decide to vote into office a chairman with much more personality than leadership ability.

In the author's opinion, this last point raises perhaps the most serious objection against choosing department heads by process of popular election. This objection was put very specifically by one district director of instruction in California who was interviewed by the author. He asserted that strong departments will probably choose strong leadership, but weak departments, with lazy or incompetent personnel, will most likely select weak leadership, so that its teachers won't feel threatened. Consequently, this administrator has opposed the efforts of some teacher factions in his district to have their department heads chosen annually by faculty vote.

Moreover, even a strong and effective chairman could find that he has decreased stature in the eyes of his colleagues if he has been elected rather than appointed to his position. In order to win the support of his "electorate," a chairman might have to act more responsibly to his teachers than to the administration of his school and district. In such a circumstance, an elected department head has only a limited opportunity to make important contributions to a total school program.

The author could find only one district in California where department chairmen are regularly chosen by election. The job description for department heads and the procedures established for their election (and recall) in that district are included in the appendix to this book. School or district administrators in other systems who might be considering the possibility of having their subject area chairmen selected by faculty vote should examine this district's administrative regulations very carefully before arriving at a final decision.

A RECOMMENDED COMPROMISE PROCEDURE

In view of the conflicting strengths and weaknesses just cited for selection of department heads entirely by administrative appointment or entirely by faculty election, the author could not recommend either procedure for his own district. Instead, he proposed a compromise system designed to combine the advantages of appointment and election while minimizing the disadvantages of both. From the author's recommendations, the following procedures have been adopted by his district:

1. New department head positions or vacancies will be publicized district-wide, with applicants invited from every school. (This opens the opportunity for promotion to department headships to the most capable teachers in the entire district, regardless of their present school assignments.)

2. Each applicant will be interviewed by a selection board consisting of the principal of the school and one teacher for each fifteen sections or fraction thereof, elected from the department in which the chairman's position is open. (Thus, the members of the board are able to evaluate a candidate's qualifications from two standpoints: that of the administrative officer responsible for the effective operation of the entire school, and that of the staff in the department for which a leader is to be chosen.)

3. Each applicant will provide his selection board with a statement of his qualifications for the position which he is seeking. (This form shows his subject matter background and teaching experience, his reasons for seeking promotion to a department head position, and also any evidences of leadership which he might have exercised in the past.) All applicant statements will be reviewed by each member of the selection board at least 48 hours before interviews are conducted.

4. The principal will weigh carefully the evaluations and recommendations of the selection board, and

the principal will make the final recommendation from among applicants interviewed.

5.   Applicants will be accepted from within and outside of the district staff. Qualifications of the applicants for the position being equal, preference will be given to those from within the district.

This compromise procedure, which resembles in some details the system currently in operation in the Beverly Hills Unified School District, opens department head opportunities to every teacher in a district while decentralizing to the individual school level the process of screening and selecting applicants. It also allows for maximum teacher participation in the selection of department heads, while reserving to the building principal the power of final appointment (subject, of course, to district-level administrative review).

By way of contrast, the author found that the procedure for selecting department heads in one very large metropolitan school district in the San Francisco Bay area is highly centralized. Furthermore, it holds to an absolute minimum the involvement of personnel—teachers *or* administrators—at the school level. In that district, new department heads are chosen from a list of applicants who had previously applied for the position. Teachers desiring to have their names added to this eligibility list may so apply, and candidates are interviewed and evaluated at meetings held twice yearly in the district administration building. When a department head vacancy occurs, a selection committee is convened to review the applicants who have passed the initial screening and whose names appear on the candidates' list.

Interestingly, the membership of this district's selection committee emphasizes the role of the central office administrative staff in making personnel appointments. The committee is composed of the assistant superintendent for secondary schools (the district is unified, combining both elementary and high schools), the assistant superintendent for human relations, the coordinators of curriculum, personnel, and guidance services, the supervisor of senior high schools, and, finally, the principal of the school in which the vacancy exists. The committee will consider the teacher nominated from the eligibility list by that principal, but it may choose to appoint another candidate altogether. In such cases, the committee does refer its choice to the principal for an interview (particularly if the principal has never met the man before), but its final decision need not be influenced by the opinions which the principal expresses concerning his new chairman's suitability. As a result, it is quite possible that a principal in that district will find assigned to his school a department head with whom he cannot work effectively. One can only guess at the consequences which such a situation has for that school's morale and instructional effectiveness!

DEFINING THE CHAIRMAN'S QUALIFICATIONS

Regardless of the method of selection finally established within a district, administrators on all levels must exercise care to insure that only applicants who are well-qualified will be chosen to become department heads. Some of the following recommendations might help districts to set minimal standards for determining which teachers are eligible for promotion to become chairmen in their schools.

Certainly, all candidates need to have more than just successful teaching experience (with or without seniority in a particular department). They must also demonstrate that they possess training and skills appropriate to their subject areas and to the positions of leadership for which they are applying.

How much academic preparation should department head applicants have? In one survey report, administrators recommended that department heads should have substantial education beyond the bachelor's degree (17.5 hours in education courses and 30 hours in courses in the subject field). Department heads contacted in the same survey recommended slightly less graduate training (13.5 hours and 26.3 hours respectively in education and the subject area) than did the administrators. However, majorities in both groups favored the master's degree for chairmen, and approximately a third of each group felt that chairmen should hold supervisory certificates.[8] This formal training provides department heads with the necessary background on which to draw while leading instructional programs in their schools.

Each candidate should also be able to demonstrate his ability to work with and lead adults, for a department head is of necessity a "teacher of teachers." This means that he will need to possess a reasonably pleasant personality, an open and inquiring mind, and emotional stability. Without these qualities—and a willingness to work hard at the job—the candidate probably will not ever become a truly effective school department head.

The job descriptions for department heads which appear in the appendix list some of the other qualifications which school districts in various parts of the nation have set for their department heads.

ESTABLISHING A TRAINING PROGRAM FOR CHAIRMEN

Once a department head has been selected to fill a vacancy, school and district administrators must immediately take steps to provide him with the kind of training which he requires if he is to work effectively in his new position. In the author's opinion, it is indefensible—professionally and economically—for a district to appoint a teacher to fill a position as complex and demanding as that of the department head and then simply to leave him there to shift for himself as best he can.

Unfortunately, however, the author noted a general absence of any kind of effective, systematic, and on-going training program for new or veteran department heads in the school districts which he visited as part of his project. When asked about such programs, administrators again and again either admitted that none existed or else expressed the hope that some sort of "training" was provided in monthly department head meetings within each school.

In reality, though, the agendas of these meetings usually show that little or no training is being provided. They tend to emphasize the operational responsibilities of department chairmen without providing any instruction in desirable ways of meeting those responsibilities. As a result, the chairmen with whom the author spoke reported that they usually left such sessions feeling overwhelmed by the demands being placed on their time and talents and also frustrated by the realization of how poorly trained they were for coping with such demands. When chairmen did ask for specific direction, they were usually told to consult the men who had held their positions before them: "Go find out from Joe how he handled that." But those that took this advice often just learned undesirable and outmoded methods of operation which they then proceeded to perpetuate in their own behaviors—with the best intentions possible. The waste of time and resources caused by the absence of effective training programs for department heads should be cause for concern among administrative staffs in each of these districts.

How can a district avoid this kind of gap in the preparation of its own department heads? What are the essential elements in a training program for both new and experienced chairmen?

A logical beginning to such a program is the creation of a job description for the position, in which the chairman's areas of responsibility are clearly defined. Then administrators on all levels should work together to help their chairmen learn how to discharge their duties as effectively as possible. This will require that they provide department heads with the kind of guidance that was detailed in Part One of this book. Beyond this, however, there are more general policies and practices which the author recommends as a means of providing organized training to all chairmen, regardless of their subject fields. The author urges that these proposals receive careful study in any district which seriously undertakes to improve the position of its chairmen.

As a first step in his training program, each newly-appointed department head should be provided an opportunity to observe how his counterparts operate in schools *other than his own.* This can be accomplished by assigning the new man to spend two or three days visiting other schools in his district, or, if possible, outstanding schools in other districts.

While visiting these schools, the new chairman should confer with the principals and with department heads in his subject area, to learn of the procedures which they have established for maintaining and improving their departmental programs. Much of value can be gained from discussions of this kind. A new appointee can be alerted, for example, to certain kinds of problems with which he will have to deal in his own school. These problems might concern personnel or the instructional materials and techniques used in that department's classrooms. The new chairman can expect to see innovations in staff utilization or curriculum development which could perhaps be adapted into his own departmental situation. Even if the visitor simply inspects the facilities available in the other schools, he will be able to learn a great deal from the experience. In any case, he will broaden his own perspectives and prepare himself to look for fresh, new approaches to providing leadership within his department.

What does a policy such as this cost a district? Actually, the expense is minimal: the salaries of substitute teachers employed tc cover the department head's classes while he is engaged in the visitations, and perhaps some very modest travel costs. By contrast the value of such training experiences as this is very great for the department head himself and also for the teachers and administrators in his school.

CONDUCTING IN-SERVICE TRAINING ACTIVITIES

Following this initial orientation to the problems and potentialities of his new assignment, the chairman must become involved in a regular program of in-service training activities within his own school. These should occur as frequently as administrators and the department heads themselves judge desirable.

An example of such an activity is "team observation." It involves the school principal as well as his department heads. Here, the principal and a group of his chairmen (preferably balanced between beginners and old hands) spend a period together visiting the class of a teacher in the school and then comparing their evaluations of what they have observed. This procedure is particularly instructive when the teacher to be visited is also a department head in the school.

In the discussion following the observation, the administrator and his chairmen have an opportunity to comment on aspects of the classroom situation which seemed desirable or undesirable, as each person perceived them. From this experience, the department heads gain increased appreciation of the highly subjective nature of classroom evaluations. Thus they see the importance of each department's having clearly-defined and measurable educational objectives if supervisors and teachers are ever going to agree on their assessment of classroom performance. In team observation activities, the newly-appointed chairman is able to note some of the kinds of things which the more experienced members of the group looked for while evaluating the classroom situation. These might include the overall condition and appearance of the room, the degree to which the teacher and the students shared in the learning process (this can be an appropriate moment for introducing a new chairman to the principles and techniques of interaction analysis), and so on through what would certainly be a lengthy list of items. And the chairman whose own teaching is observed by such a team is reminded of how differently a classroom situation may sometimes appear to a teacher working in front of a group and to another teacher observing from the rear of the room. Such a reminder can help him in his future work with instructors in his own department.

Another example of this kind of practical, on-the-job training activity is "resource center analysis." In this operation, a principal and his department heads convene one afternoon in a selected departmental office, to study the ways in which the chairman working in that office has organized the room to serve as an efficient resource and management center for his department. The chairman serving as host for the meeting should point out how he has equipped the office with teaching resources which are appropriate to his subject field and readily available to his teachers. Or he could demonstrate the systems which he follows in handling the managerial functions of his position. From such visits as this, the other department heads—new and experienced—learn ways in which they can reorganize their own offices and office procedures to achieve greater efficiency.

On a broader scale, an excellent source of training for department heads is the creation and use of an operations manual for chairmen in a particular subject field. Curriculum manuals for teachers are now fairly common in many schools, but leadership manuals such as suggested here are not, and they can make a major contribution to the improvement of department head performance.

A district can profitably undertake to produce such a manual for chairmen in a selected subject area on a pilot, experimental basis. If subsequent evaluation shows that the handbook has proved useful, the district should authorize the publication of similar manuals for department heads in other subject fields, as rapidly as funds permit. Experience should prove that a manual, or parts of a manual, can serve chairmen in more than one subject, in which case the cost of a program such as this is lessened.

The writing of the manual should be assigned to two or three department heads in the selected curricular area, who meet together for discussion and writing during a summer workshop. In their book, the chairmen should draw on their training and experience to discuss desirable practices in situations which they typically encounter while performing their duties as department heads. These could include supervision of instruction, curriculum development, and departmental management, any of the kinds of responsibility surveyed in the first part of this book. The writers should also be asked to include a discussion of ways in which the instructional programs carried on in their subject can be better coordinated with the programs presented in other departments in their schools. Such guidelines as these are invaluable in a school whose administrators were working to encourage more inter-disciplinary teaching activities.

The foregoing have only been suggestions for the kinds of training which districts must provide for department heads on a school or district-wide basis. The author believes that once a program of this kind is initiated, additional ideas for training activities will be proposed by the administrators and chairmen who participate in it.

Additional opportunities for carrying on the kind of in-service training work which allows a district to better utilize the leadership potentiality of its department head staff are discussed in Chapters 7, 8, and 9 of this book.

RECEIVING TRAINING THROUGH TRANSFERS

After a chairman has served in his position in a particular school for a number of years, administrators in his district should plan to include in his training program an experience which allows him to leave his position and assume other responsibilities in a new situation for a semester or two. This has the effect of further broadening his perspective on his work as departmental leader. Such an experience can be provided by periodically transferring experienced department heads to short-term teaching-observation assignments in other schools in their district.

To illustrate how this procedure operates, consider the following hypothetical example.

A veteran social studies department head in School X is given a semester or year's leave from his duties in that school and transferred to the social studies department in School Y. There he does not serve as chairman; his lack of familiarity with the personnel and programs in that school severely limits his ability to exercise effective leadership there. Instead, he serves as a regular classroom teacher. Ideally, he has a reduced teaching load in the new school, with perhaps an hour assigned as a "conference-observation" period. This released time coincides with the periods when the regular chairman of the social studies department in School Y is free from teaching responsibilities. This provides them an opportunity in which to discuss their respective departmental programs in detail and to carry out cooperative activities which make maximum use of the visiting chairman's ability and experience. During the period of his service in the new school, the transferred chairman (who might carry the title or rank of "Visting Teacher Specialist") attends all social studies department meetings, faculty meetings, and department head councils in that school, to observe and to participate as requested.

What benefits can the transferred department head expect to derive from this experience? They resemble in nature—but to a greater depth—the benefits received by the newly-appointed chairman who spends a day or two visiting another school in his district or elsewhere in his state. The transfer gives him an opportunity to examine in detail a department which undoubtedly operates with different policies and materials than he is accustomed to. He should discover that certain aspects of these new programs could be incorporated into his own department. He also has an opportunity to observe the leadership techniques employed by the principal and department heads in his host school; again, he might wish to adopt some of these for himself. And finally, by virtue of this short sabbatical from his administrative responsibilities, he can gain some valuable new perceptions concerning department head–teacher relationships.

This kind of transfer program offers other worthwhile results for a district beyond the training that the visiting chairman receives, valuable as that is in itself. The transferred chairman has a contribution of his own to make to his host school, where he serves as an important resource person and consultant to the administrators and teachers in that school. Moreover, his vacancy in his own school has been filled (and the personnel levels in the two departments balanced) by the transfer of a social studies teacher in school Y to serve temporarily in school X. This provides for excellent two-way communication between the two schools, inasmuch as this teacher now has an opportunity to familiarize himself with the programs and policies established in School X. Upon his return to his regular school after the conclusion of the transfer period, this instructor will report on his experiences and recommend that his own school adopt any of the materials or policies which impressed him during his stay at School X. There is a final benefit for the department head position to be realized from this transfer policy. That is the creation of a reserve of personnel with some training and experience to fill future department head vacancies in the district. These potential future chairmen are the teachers who have been selected to serve as chairmen during the periods when the regular department heads are away from their schools on transfers. Thus, to continue the illustration above, the principal of School X needs to appoint a temporary social studies chairman during the semester or year that the regular chairman is away. He will undoubtedly fill this vacancy from among the most promising experienced teachers in the staff of that department. While occupying the chairman's position, this teacher receives valuable training and experience, and he can be expected to apply for the next social studies department head vacancy to occur in the district.

Admittedly, this policy of training by transfer imposes additional demands on the schools and personnel involved. For this reason, the practice cannot be applied with equal facility in all subject areas, especially not in smaller departments where teachers work in very highly specialized areas and where a transfer such as that discussed here could seriously upset an instructional program.

However, in larger departments such as English, social studies, mathematics, foreign languages, business education, and physical education, where there is more flexibility in individual teacher assignments, the periodic transfers of department heads can provide important benefits to the schools, departments, and staff concerned.

REQUIRING ACADEMIC TRAINING

The training which department heads should receive through administrative direction ought to extend beyond the kinds of practical, on-the-job activities described thus far in this chapter. Good chairmen are more than imitators of successful practices which they are provided opportunities to observe; they must be able to develop innovative practices of their own. To do this effectively, they need to be familiar with fundamental concepts of curriculum development and instructional supervision, which will provide them with guidelines for their individual activities.

Districts which are establishing training programs, for department heads as an initial step toward improving the position should, therefore, consider the advisability of requiring that their chairmen receive formal instruction in the areas of program and personnel management. Such a policy can begin by requiring that within a set period of time (perhaps three years) following his appointment, every chairman must furnish evidence that he has completed at least one college or university course, or one approved workshop, in the theories and practices of providing leadership in his field. If subsequent evaluation of this requirement demonstrates that it has led to improved performance on the part of the district's department heads, then additional courses or workshops should be required periodically thereafter (perhaps once every three to five years) as a prerequisite for continued appointment to department head positions.

It is the author's opinion, based on his own experiences and the recommendations of the many administrators, department chairmen, and teachers with whom he conferred during the course of his study, that supervision should receive the primary emphasis in this required academic preparation. Far too many department heads who regularly engage in supervisory activities have had little or no preparation for this critically important work. Depending on the needs and wishes of a particular district, this training in the area of supervision might be defined narrowly, or it might be broadened to include sensitivity training or instruction in group dynamics or interaction analysis.

SUMMARY

As a first step toward designing a program to improve the department head position in any district, we have considered the procedures by which new chairmen are selected. We weighed the advantages and disadvantages of designating department heads by administrative appointment or by teacher election. A plan which combines the advantages of both while minimizing their possible drawbacks was then recommended for adoption. The author contrasted this proposed system with the highly centralized procedures followed in one district which he visited. Finally, the recommendations of a number of administrators and department heads concerning the kind of qualification which a new chairman should possess were reported.

We next established the need for a systematic and on-going training program for both new and experienced chairmen, in order to make the most effective use of their talents. We saw how this training can be provided through visitations, in-service activity programs, leadership manuals, and academic preparation.

With good selection and training procedures established, any district will have taken major steps toward improving the position and performance of its department heads. In the next chapters, we will consider the kinds of efficient operational conditions which districts should provide for their chairmen after they have been selected and trained.

7

Supporting Department Heads
with Necessary
Time and Money

Time *is* money, in education as in business, but the top-flight department head needs both to carry on his work effectively. He needs time in which to meet his many curricular and managerial responsibilities. And he needs the incentive provided by salary increments if he is to continue to meet those responsibilities effectively year after year.

In this chapter, we will study the problem that school districts face in providing time and money for their subject area chairmen. We will also see how this problem is being solved—even in districts with low tax bases.

"Released time from classroom teaching assingments should be a condition of employment (for department heads) rather than a compensation for the assignment. Financial compensation alone cannot substitute for released time since inadequate time, regardless of the reason, limits the (chairman's) opportunity to visit classes, confer with teachers, conduct demonstration lessons, and administer departmental affairs...The amount of time that department heads should be released from classroom teaching assignments is directly proportional to the number of teachers in the department and the responsibilities assigned the department head. There is no substitute for time! It is difficult to understand the rationale of establishing heads of departments if they are not provided with released time...."[9]

Every experienced department head knows the truth of that statement; he knows that without sufficient time for meeting his responsibilities, he is a departmental leader in name only. Even the most talented and well-trained chairman will experience only frustration if he does not receive the essential support of released time. But cost-conscious administrators know that released time is the most expensive kind of support which a district can be asked to provide. Depending on the existing teachers' salary schedule a single daily released period for a chairman can cost as much as $3000 annually. Thus, in a district with three or four high schools, each of which is staffed with perhaps ten or twelve chairmen, it can easily be seen that providing released time for heads of departments will require a heavy commitment of resources. This cost becomes even greater if the heads of larger departments are given more than one released hour daily, as recommended by the National Council of Teachers of English: "Each chairman should teach at least one class, but for each five teachers or major fraction thereof, he should be released one period (in addition to his regular preparation period) for duties as English department chairman."[10] The logic underlying this recommendation is self-evident. In large high schools, departments such as English and social studies resemble small schools in themselves, with staffs of twenty or more teachers in each. Such organizations are far too large and complex for one individual to supervise effectively during just one period each day. And yet the heavy cost of providing this much released time is also self-evident.

Ideally, every district would be financially capable of providing sufficient released time for all of its department heads and would recognize that this investment of its resources is an essential prerequisite to developing and maintaining quality leadership in each subject field. However, the hard fact is that many school systems are unable to meet such costs. What are administrators in such districts to do? Must they resign themselves to an annual search for teachers who can be urged to take on the duties and responsibilities of the department headship as an extra-curricular assignment? Must they be content to accept the grudging and uninspired "leadership" that chairmen give in such a situation?

In the next few pages, we will examine several plans by which administrators in districts which cannot afford regular released periods for their chairmen can provide at least a minimum of essential time for their support. These will be compromise plans at best, but they offer some alternative to the kind of critical situation which the author found prevailing in some of the districts which he visited.

These recommendations can also provide administrators in more fortunate districts with a means of supplementing the released time which they already provide their chairmen. This additional time can be used to free the department heads in one school each year for a day or two of intensive, cooperative planning for long-range inter-disciplinary curriculum improvements.

PROVIDING RELEASED TIME—PERIODICALLY

One compromise plan provides a regular released period for heads of larger departments, in recognition of the heavy demands placed upon them for continuous planning and supervision with their staffs, while heads of smaller departments are given released time on a periodic basis. This time is made available whenever their departmental responsibilities become most demanding. In the event that a district is unable to meet the costs of a regular released hour for even the heads of larger departments, the same policy of providing periodic free time can be extended to cover all chairmen. In such cases, responsible administrators should use an appropriate time/responsibility scale to increase the number of days of released time allocated to chairmen with larger staffs to direct.

Periodic releases from classroom teaching duties can be provided in several ways. In one situation, a district budgets a sum of money sufficient to give every department head a specified number of days of substitute teacher time annually. Each chairman selects the days on which the substitutes are called in to relieve him of his classes.

From a district's point of view, this plan makes it possible to provide department heads with some essential time at a fraction of the cost of a released period daily. Allowing each chairman just ten days of substitute teacher services annually frees him from his classes for a total of two full weeks during the school year, at perhaps a tenth of the cost of providing even a single released hour daily.

Department heads can, of course, find much to criticize in a compromise such as this. They know that substitute teachers rarely provide the quality of instruction that they or another regular teacher can offer their students. Chairmen also know that teachers are not totally "freed" from their classroom responsibilities when substitute teachers are called in, for they still have to make plans for the substitutes to follow during their absences. And after their return, they still must grade the papers or projects which their students prepared under the substitutes' direction.

On the other hand, administrators can be sure that chairmen will find this compromise more attractive than the prospect of having no released time at all. Administrators should point out that during the days when they are released from their classes, the chairmen can conduct formal in-class supervision of their teachers. They will also have time on those days to take care of such duties as ordering supplies and equipment, preparing departmental budgets or teaching schedules, and planning for future curriculum improvement projects.

Administrators can also help their chairmen to find ways in which the use of substitute teachers will not lessen the quality of instruction provided in their classes, nor place extra burdens on the chairmen themselves. This can be accomplished if substitutes are brought in on days when a department head's students require a minimum amount of teacher direction in carrying on their classroom work. Such a day would be one during which films are to be shown to the class, so that the substitute is responsible only for introducing the films and leading class discussion after they have been presented. Or again, substitutes can be called in when a class is going to spend an hour reading or working on laboratory or classroom projects of an essentially self-directing nature.

Another plan for providing department heads with periodic released time makes extensive use of teaching teams. By scheduling a chairman to participate in as many teaching teams as possible, school administrators make it possible for him to provide in-class supervision of his staff every day. And when necessary, a chairman who is part of a team can leave his classes for varying periods of time without depriving his students of the benefits of instruction from a regular teacher, as opposed to a substitute teacher. This plan has the disadvantage of placing additional burdens on the other teachers in each team whenever the chairman must be absent, so administrators might do well to consider this as a supplement rather than an alternative to a policy of providing periodic released time through the use of substitutes, as described above. As a supplement, the team teaching plan increases the number of options open to department heads who occasionally need short and uninterrupted periods of time in which to deal with particular departmental responsibilities.

NON-CERTIFICATED ASSISTANCE FOR CHAIRMEN

Once a district has adopted policies which, to the best of its available resources, provide time for department heads to carry out their duties, then administrators in that district must see that the time provided is properly used. If capable, conscientious individuals have been appointed to department head positions, if they clearly understand their duties and are properly trained to discharge them, then districts may be reasonably confident that their chairmen will not *want* to waste the time that is given them for their work.

In actuality, however, much of this time may be wasted if department heads are not given sufficient non-certificated assistance to relieve them of petty, routine responsibilities. Again quoting the study of outstanding departments conducted by the National Council of Teachers of English: "Even with released time, (the chairman's) responsibilities should not include typing letters, reports, and book orders, mimeographing, cataloging, and the myriad of other clerical tasks that so often fall to the chairman...Every English department should be given part-time professional clerical help and in a large department (fifteen or more teachers) full-time clerical help should be available."[11] This same recommendation applies equally in other subject area departments, in the author's opinion.

Thus, it becomes essential that district and school administrators periodically review their policies regarding allocation of clerical and other non-certificated services within each school. It is an appalling waste of tax dollars and teacher talent to release a master teacher at the top of a district's salary schedule from part of his classroom duties in order to have him perform routine clerical duties—and usually perform them far less effectively than a secretary earning a fraction of his salary. Similarly, physical education chairmen who must spend time counting towels are being misused, as are industrial arts chairmen who have to uncrate their own tools, or science and art department heads who must count their own supplies.

What is the alternative? Some of these duties could be assigned to secretaries, while others should become the responsiblity of school custodians. Or, just as many districts now make use of community volunteers or part-time paraprofessionals to grade papers or assist in remedial classes, so they might recruit such aides to take over many of the routine duties now being performed by department heads.

In one suburban high school near San Francisco, the author found a teacher aide working at least part-time in every department office. These assistants handled most departmental paper work—distributing and answering correspondence, typing memos and orders, filing, etc.—and also performed general secretarial services for the other teachers in the departments to which they were assigned. Needless to say, the teachers and administrators in that school were very enthusiastic about this kind of support. The teacher aide program in this school was not only highly effective, in terms of providing essential services, but it was also surprisingly inexpensive. For the most part, the aides were housewives from the community who welcomed a chance to work in the schools for a few hours each day, at a very modest salary. They were paid less than $3 per hour for their services, and at this figure, even a full-time aide, working six hours daily for the entire school year, costs the district less than $3000 annually.

Another way to provide non-certificated assistance for

department heads is through the use of students from "office training" classes. Many schools visited by the author have established such classes in their business education departments. Students who enroll in this subject are assigned to work stations in department offices, where they put to practical use the skills which they learned in typing, shorthand, bookkeeping, and other business education classes. Such assignments provide valuable, on-the-job training for the students, who may rotate from office to office during the school year. They also relieve department heads of many routine managerial tasks—at no cost to their districts—and thus free them to devote themselves to improving instruction and developing curriculum in their departments.

IMPROVING DEPARTMENT HEAD SALARIES

Every district must be prepared to extend appropriate financial recognition to its department heads if it expects to attract its most capable teachers to the position and then to hold them there. Some teachers, it is true, may seek department head appointments because they value the prestige that the position carries or the opportunity it provides to spend part of the school day working with adults on a policy-making level. But few applicants will be found willing to give the position the continuous time and effort it requires unless they find it as rewarding financially as it can be professionally.

How much additional salary should department heads receive, and on what basis? This is the critical question confronting administrators who wish to make the chairman's position in their district competitive with that in other, comparable systems.

Special compensation for department heads usually takes one of two forms: through a separate salary schedule or through payment of an increment above the regular teachers' salary schedule. In the next few pages, we will see how these policies are applied in a number of districts in California and other parts of the country.

Many districts have preferred to establish uniform, graduated salary schedules for all department heads, rewarding experience in the position just as it is usually rewarded in the salary schedules adopted for administrators and teachers. As an example, department heads in the San Francisco Unified School District are placed on a single, five-step pay scale, regardless of the number of teachers in their respective departments (above the minimum required for the establishment of a department head position in the first place). In 1968, this scale ranged from $390 to $1415 above the regular teachers' salary levels.

Other districts have compensated their chairmen for their additional responsibilities by means of increments which vary according to the size of the department, the nature of the duties assigned each chairman, and similar factors. As an example of this procedure, chairmen in the Claremont Unified School District, near Los Angeles, were paid an additional $100 in 1968 for each teacher in their departments. As a result, the increments paid to department heads in that system vary widely.

What is the picture on a national level?

A survey of department head policies was conducted in 443 school systems which had reported an enrollment of over 12,000 in the previous fall. Responses were received from 403 systems, or 88 percent of the total. The survey revealed the following practices in effect in regard to salaries paid to department heads:

"Of the 250 systems reporting the employment of department heads, 66 place these personnel on the classroom teacher's salary schedule, with no extra compensation. However, 32 of this group grant their department heads released time or a lighter teaching load, to allow time for their additional duties.

"The remaining 184 systems pay their department heads a higher salary than that received by classroom teachers. Four of these systems indicated that department heads have released time or a lighter teaching load, in addition to extra compensation. The various methods which are used to determine the salaries of department heads are described below.

"In 18 systems, department heads are paid on a separate salary schedule, distinct from classroom teachers. Seven of these systems furnished information on salaries for department heads at the bachelor's degree level; 11 furnished information on salaries for this position at the master's degree level. No system sent in a complete salary schedule for this position. The mean bachelor's degree maximum in the systems with separate schedules is $8357.

At the master's degree level, the mean of the maximums is $10,167.

"In 166 systems (two-thirds of the total number of systems reporting the use of department heads) these personnel are paid a differential over the regular classroom teachers' salary which would be appropriate to their preparation and length of service. This differential may be calculated in a variety of ways:

> "In 68 systems, it is a flat sum—the same to all department heads. The range of these sums, in the 68 systems, is from $100 to $1100, the mean differential paid in this manner is $377, and half of the flat-sum differentials fall between $275 and $530 per year.

> "A flat percent is paid by an additional 22 systems; 18 of these percents are equally distributed between 3 and 14 percent of the annual salary; the remaining four are 18 percent, 19 percent, 23 percent, and 25 percent, respectively.

> "Some respondents listed a range of differentials used within their systems to pay department heads—$100 to $600, or 4 percent to 12 percent, for example. Placement within the range in these systems is determined by such factors as the length of service as department head, the number of teachers in the department, and the number of hours spent coordinating the work of the department.

"Summarized in the diagram below are the major methods of calculating salary differentials for department heads. Of the 166 systems paying differentials, 136 are accounted for in this summary.

"In the remaining 30 school systems, the method of calculating the department head differential takes a variety of forms, some of which deserve mention:

> "In some cases, the differential is a fixed amount per teacher in the department—$2.50 per month per teacher; or such a per-teacher supplement may be added to a base amount—$400, plus $10 per teacher in the department, on an annual basis.

	DOLLAR DIFFERENTIALS	PERCENT OR RATIO DIFFERENTIALS
FIXED AMOUNTS	Number of systems = 68 Range of differential = $100 to $1100 Mean = $377	Number of systems = 22 Range of differential = 3% to 25% Mean = 8.4%
VARIABLE AMOUNTS	Number of systems = 40 Range of extremes = $100 to $2125 Mean of midpoints = $375	Number of systems = 6 Range of extremes = 2% to 30% Mean of midpoints = 11.8%

"Sliding scales may also be used. For example, in one system, the head of a department comprising fewer than four teachers will get a differential of $105; if the department contains four to six teachers, $147; seven to nine teachers, $186; and if the department head supervises 10 teachers or more, the differential is $216.

"In other cases, the number of class sections, rather than the number of teachers, determines the extra compensation of the department head—a $75 minimum, plus $5 per class section, in one case; $18 per class in the department, in another.

"One system solves the problem of extra pay for department heads by advancing each individual one increment on the teacher's salary schedule.

"Index ratios are used by some systems to determine compensation for department heads. As an example, the ratio formula used by Fresno, California, is reproduced...

FRESNO, CALIFORNIA

Additional Service Pay Schedule for Department Chairmen

A department chairman, when so designated by the principal,

will be paid according to the following additional service pay schedule:

1. Responsibility index: 12 for each department.

2. Time index, to be determined by the principal, as follows:

Total hours for activity above normal teaching load	Index	Total hours for activity above normal teaching load	Index
Less than 60	1	100-120	6
60-70	2	120-140	7
70-80	3	140-160	8
80-90	4	160-180	9
90-100	5	180-200 or more	10

3. Size of department index (determined from the previous year's schedule of classes):

Number of classes in the department	6-20	21-40	41-60	61-80	81-100	101-120
Size Index	5	6	7	8	9	10

4. The three numbers (responsibility index, time index, and size of department index) added, equal the TOTAL INDEX, which gives the amount of remuneration as follows:

TOTAL INDEX	Differential	TOTAL INDEX	Differential	TOTAL INDEX	Differential
1 4 or less	$ 50	21	$150	27	$300
15	60	22	175	28	325
16	70	23	200	29	350
17	80	24	225	30	375
18	90	25	250	31	400
19	100	26	275	32	425
20	125				

"To compare the salaries of regular classroom teachers and department heads, the Educational Research Service prepared (the following) table. Data for department head salaries are from the postal card inquiry; teachers' salary data for each of the systems reporting department heads were taken from the NEA Research Division's report of the 19___-___ salary schedules for classroom teachers, footnoted at the bottom of the table. All systems reporting salary information were included in the tabulations regardless of whether their department heads were paid the same salaries as teachers, received a differential above the teacher's salary appropriate to them, or were paid on a spearate schedule. In cases where a range was given for a department head salary, the midpoint of the range was selected as the most typical figure. Since not all the systems having department heads submitted salary information, Columns 2 and 4 of (the table) show the number of systems included in the means for each stratum.

"As can be seen....a typical high school department head earns nearly $400 per year more than a teacher in the same system with comparable education and experience. There is wide variation between strata in the amount department heads are paid, at the various salary schedule points."

A COMPARISON BETWEEN MEAN SCHEDULED MAXIMUM SALARIES FOR CLASSROOM TEACHERS AND DEPARTMENT HEADS

Position	Bachelor's degree level		Master's degree level	
	Number of systems [a]	Mean of maximums	Number of systems [a]	Mean of maximums
1	2	3	4	5
Stratum 1 (over 100,000 enrollment)	16	$	18	$
Department heads		8478		9454
Teachers[b]		8272		9043
Difference		206		411
Stratum 2 (50,000 to 99,999 enrollment)	25		27	
Department heads		7887		8725
Teachers[b]		7559		8427
Difference		328		298

Stratum 3 (25,000 to 49,999 enrollment) 32		35
Department heads	8219	9115
Teachers[b/]	7874	8767
Difference	345	348
Stratum 4 (12,000 to 24,999 enrollment) 126		144
Department heads	7983	8985
Teachers[b/]	7560	8495
Difference	423	490
Overall means (Strata 1-4) 199		224
Department heads	8049	8971
Teachers[b/]	7667	8574
Difference	382	397

[a/] Data on salaries were not submitted by all systems reporting the employment of department heads.

[b/] Classroom teachers' salary data for systems having department heads taken from: NEA Research Division. *Salary Schedules for Classroom Teachers, 1965-66* Research Report 1965-R15, October 1965.[12]

As these figures show, there are marked differences in the actual amounts of extra compensation which districts award to their department heads. These differences reflect, at least in part, variations in the financial resources available to school systems in different parts of the country. The survey demonstrates, however, that there is widespread acceptance of the principle that chairmen do deserve higher salaries, in recognition of their increased responsibilities.

Administrators who are looking for other bench marks on which to base their own district policies should consult the appendix to this book. There they will find a survey of policies relating to extra pay for department heads in public junior and senior high schools in the state of California.

ESTABLISHING PERFORMANCE BONUSES

Regardless of which of the above methods a district may

choose for determining extra compensation for department heads, the author also urges administrators in every district to study the possibility of rewarding the most capable and creative chairmen with an additional performance bonus.

This recommendation is made in the full knowledge that any proposal to evaluate performance as a basis for compensation is certain to engender heated controversy in most educational circles.

Many school boards and many administrators support the concept of "merit pay" because it enables a district to use the money which it has budgeted for salary purposes more selectively than is now possible where compensation must be applied uniformly. Such selectivity allows a district to attract and hold truly outstanding teachers, and keep them in the classroom where they are most effective. Teachers, on the other hand, are generally skeptical about "merit pay." They tend to raise the very practical question of who is qualified to do the evaluating of their performance with consistent objectivity and against what accepted criteria of "good" teaching.

The author suggests that it is possible for a district to use selective compensation policies effectively by first applying them only to department heads. It can base these rewards on the results of annual evaluations of their performance *as department heads.* In Chapter 10, the author will propose that all department heads be evaluated annually as a means of improving their performance. Further, it will be suggested that the evaluation be based upon the job description established for the position, so that the criteria for determining effective performance will be clearly defined. Finally, it will be recommended that the evaluation be conducted from three levels, so that the most complete and accurate estimate of a chairman's effectiveness can be compiled. Specifically, the recommendation will call for each department head to be evaluated by the teachers in his department, by himself (through his own annual report on his work), and by his administrative superiors.

The author believes that it should be possible for an evaluation staff (comprised perhaps of administrators, department heads, and teachers) to study these evaluations, to make allowance for differences in the conditions under which chairmen in each school work, and then to arrive at fair and reasonable comparisons of their performances. Where these evaluations indicate that a chairman has satisfactorily carried out the duties specified in his job description and has gone substantially beyond those duties, to undertake additional activities leading to the improvement of his department, he should receive additional compensation.

At the present time, the author does not know whether this plan will work effectively with the chairmen in any given school district. And it is certainly debatable whether such a plan, even if it did work, could be extended to apply equally well to the rest of the staff in that district. The author is reasonably certain, however, that "merit pay" is a dead issue if even a limited plan such as he proposes here does *not* work.

SUMMARY

In this chapter, we reviewed some of the thorniest problems confronting administrators who seek ways to improve the conditions under which department heads in their schools work:

1. How much released time should department heads receive—and how can this district afford to give it?

2. How can we free department heads from the routine tasks that consume so much of their time and energy?

3. How much extra salary do our chairmen deserve?

To answer these questions, we examined some innovative proposals for giving department heads released time on at least a periodic basis. We also saw how secretaries, teacher aides, and business education students can assist chairmen by relieving them of clerical responsibilities in their offices. Finally, we examined representative salary policies and schedules for department heads from all parts of the country—and considered the possibility of supplementing these schedules with performance bonuses.

8

Helping Department Heads
Work Together
More Effectively
in the School and District

It is a common practice for administrators in the modern secondary school to call their department heads together for consultation on a more or less regular basis. At these "first Monday of the month" conferences in the principal's office, the assembled chairmen provide the specific information concerning course offerings, teaching resources and strategies, and staff and facility utilization that administrators need in order to plan and direct a total school program.

Similarly, on a district level, the department heads in each subject area are occasionally brought together from their individual schools to serve as an advisory council for the district superintendent and his staff. A superintendent or curriculum director may refer to such a panel of experts for information concerning research or current practices in their subject field. The council may also simply be asked to share information among its members concerning the work of their individual departments, to improve communication and coordination among schools in the district.

The author is convinced that such meetings as these do not begin to utilize the full potential of the department head position for providing information and leadership on a school or district level. It is true that useful work is accomplished at such routine rounds of meetings, but districts which select, train, and support competent chairmen can derive far greater benefits from their collected knowledge and experience. To accomplish this, such districts will have to find ways to help department heads meet and work together in a truly professional and executive manner.

In this chapter, administrators will find a number of proposals which can provide just such opportunities for their department heads, both during the regular school year and the summer vacation period.

SCHEDULING CONCURRENT RELEASED TIME

A principal who wishes to have his chairmen work together more closely and cooperatively can begin by arranging their teaching schedules so that their preparation and/or released periods coincide during the school day. Ideally, the department heads will be free from classroom duties during the last period or two in the afternoon; if this is not possible, then they should be scheduled to a common released hour early in the morning or just before lunch. In any case, such a policy of arranging for concurrent released or preparation time makes it easy for the principal or his administrative assistants to call the chairmen together quickly for discussions of school policies and practices. No longer is it necessary to wait until the regular monthly department head meeting—a dreary relic from the past—or to call special meetings for the late afternoon, at a time when everyone is free but when creative energies are at their lowest. Instead, the principal can call his staff together for frequent, perhaps weekly meetings of shorter duration, with very timely and specific agendas to consider. And when it does become necessary to hold longer sessions, when curriculum development and coordination must be discussed at greater length, the participants will find that the earlier starting time allows them to accomplish much more within a given number of hours.

Having released periods which coincide at some point in the

day also tends to encourage individual department heads to work together on a more frequent, if informal, basis. A chairman who has an idea concerning ways in which his department's programs can be better integrated with those in another department knows that his colleague from the other department is readily available to discuss the plan with him from the very beginning. Thus, a music chairman, whose work usually keeps him in a separate part of the campus, away from his counterpart in social studies, finds it very easy to meet with the other since both are free at the same time. Out of their discussion might come plans for the presentation of a short unit on music history in certain social studies classes. From this will come not only an enrichment of the school's history program but also a stimulation of student interest in music and music department courses. This kind of exchange benefits both departments and serves as an important step toward the better integration of the educational experiences of students enrolled in that school.

One example of how a creative administrator has used the policy of concurrent released time to help his department heads meet and work together with unusual effectiveness is to be found in the Henry M. Gunn Senior High School in Palo Alto, California. On this modern, functional campus, all curriculum associates (as chairmen are designated in that district) are released from afternoon teaching assignments. This enables them to meet together frequently with administrators in the school, to discuss all aspects of the functioning of their individual departments. In the opinion of the principal and the associates alike, some of the most productive of these conferences take place in the regular Thursday afternoon meetings devoted to "curriculum." (Rather interestingly, the principal of the school has chosen this term to describe the kind of instructional program that the school plans to offer three, five, or ten years in the future.) The author did not find this kind of highly creative, long-range planning occurring on such a regular and sustained basis in any of the other schools which he visited during the course of his study. Much of the credit for achieving such a high level of effective administrator-department head cooperation undoubtedly belongs to the gifted individuals who comprise the leadership staff in this particular school. The author is convinced, however, that the policy of concurrent released time provides the framework which makes such achievement possible, and that this same framework can be established in most secondary schools of at least medium size.

VARYING THE LOCATION OF
DEPARTMENT HEAD MEETINGS

As another step toward improving communication and coordination among his department heads, a principal should plan to schedule his meetings with his chairmen to take place in different parts of the school, rotating these settings from department to department.

The author believes that administrators who still schedule their department head meetings, whether weekly or monthly, to take place in a single, set place within their schools are missing an excellent opportunity to make the meeting place itself an instructive part of the agenda. It is true that a large, centrally located classroom or a faculty dining room provides a convenient place in which to hold meetings with chairmen, but much more benefit can be derived by scheduling the meetings to convene perhaps in a reading laboratory one month, a history classroom the next, and then a homemaking kitchen, industrial arts shop, and so forth after that. In a crowded building, where classroom facilities are in constant use, the department head meeting could begin in a selected teaching station at noon and then be shifted to the principal's office or faculty lounge when afternoon classes began. This, of course, presupposes that concurrent released periods have been scheduled for the afternoon; otherwise, the meetings could not be resumed until after the close of school that day.

In order to take full advantage of the instructional opportunities offered by this policy of rotating the location of department head meetings, administrators ought to reserve a part of the time at every meeting for a discussion led by the chairman in whose area the group has convened. This individual takes the opportunity thus presented to discuss briefly a particular teaching practice or problem common to that room. The topic of this discussion should have been chosen earlier in conference with the principal, to insure that it is one that has important implications for classes in other subject areas. Following the comments by the "host" chairman, the principal might invite the rest of the department heads to consider how the information which they have heard or the facility in which they find themselves can be adapted for use in their own departmental programs. This practice stimulates useful discussion at the time of the meeting, and it also provides material for follow-up conferences among particular chairmen seeking ways in which to improve or integrate their curricular offerings.

Individual department heads should apply this same principle to selecting the locations of their own department meetings. Rotating meetings among the different classrooms or teaching stations within a department, with the same sort of discussion as that described above taking place, improves communication and coordination among the teachers in that department. This is a simple and direct step leading toward major improvements in each department's instructional programs.

ESTABLISHING EFFECTIVE PROCEDURES
FOR DISTRICT LEVEL MEETING

We have seen how administrators in each school can help department heads work together more effectively in their individual buildings. In the same way, district office administrators can improve the functioning of councils of chairmen drawn from each subject area to meet on a district level. An initial step in accomplishing this improvement is a review of the responsibilities assigned to these councils. After these have been clearly defined, more effective procedures can be established for helping department heads meet those responsibilties.

The following guidelines might be helpful to districts which are planning to establish councils of subject area chairmen or which are reviewing the operations of such councils already in existence.

Typically, a district council of department heads is composed of chairmen in a particular subject area, drawn from all of the district's secondary schools. In addition, an administrative liaison usually meets with each council; this individual should be a member of the superintendent's staff (a director or coordinator of curriculum and instruction), a principal, or vice-principal for curriculum selected from one of the district schools. If the administrative liaison is assigned to the council representing the subject area in which he himself formerly taught, he will probably have valuable contributions to make from his own experience when the council discusses materials and techniques of instruction. Other participants in a district council meeting might include representatives from community groups such as the PTA (on a more or less regular basis) and personnel from the district's business office, technical services department, teacher aide office, etc. (as the topics on the council agenda require their presence). Classroom teachers from that council's subject area should always be welcome, of course.

The councils should select their own officers in any manner which they deem appropriate. Each council should probably elect at least two such officers: a chairman and a secretary. The chief duties of the chairman include establishing and publishing the agenda for each council meeting (with the assistance of the administrative liaison), presiding over council sessions, and serving as the council's representative when discussing council matters with administrators and teachers in the district, as appropriate. The secretary is responsible for preparing and distributing council minutes (making sure that sufficient copies go to administrative bodies on the district and school level and to every teacher in the subject field represented by the council), and for handling correspondence between the council and administrative or faculty groups within the district.

Every council must plan to meet on a regular, scheduled basis during the school year. This provides the members with an opportunity to engage in frequent discussions of curriculum and instructional practices in their subject area and to respond quickly to questions referred to them by the superintendent and his staff. Some of these meetings can take place in the district office, as a convenience to school or central office administrators who might wish or be invited to attend. However, a council should consider the recommendation made earlier for department heads within a school: that the location of their meetings be rotated from area to area, as a means of developing their familiarity with the total school program.

Applying this recommendation on a district level, a council might plan to hold half of its meetings in the central office and to rotate the remainder from school to school in the district. Thus, one meeting of a science council, for example, takes place in a physics laboratory in School X and another meeting a month or two later in a biology classroom in School Y. This practice also serves to involve teachers other than department heads in council meetings, thus increasing the opportunity for first-hand communication among as many of the district faculty as possible. Continuing the illustration above, science chairmen who know that their next session will be held in the chemistry laboratory in School Y should invite chemistry teachers from their own departments to join them at the meeting. This gives these instructors a chance to inspect the facilities and programs for teaching their subject in a different school, to talk with other chemistry teachers in attendance at the meeting, and, if appropriate, to participate in the work of the council meeting itself.

During its regular meetings, a district subject area council might discuss or act upon a variety of matters. Some of its business will be referred to it by teachers in individual schools, for one of the major functions of each council is to reflect the thinking of teachers in that field and to act upon their recommendations. Other items for consideration typically come from the superintendent's staff or from school-level administrators, presented directly or through the administrative liaison. Naturally, many other items on a council agenda will be proposed by council members themselves, and a few might originate in state or national professional organizations which recommend adoption of educational philosophies or practices.

Among the kinds of activities which usually appear on a district council agenda are the following, presented from any of the sources listed above:

1. Definition and development of educational philos-
    ophies and curriculum in the subject field repre-
    sented by the council. This involves establishing
    the instructional objectives in the subject, select-
    ing and designing the content for courses intended
    to meet those objectives, and recommending pro-
    cedures for periodic in-depth review and improve-
    ment of the existing instructional programs (per-

haps through summer curriculum workshops directed by the council).

2. Evaluation of the instructional programs in the subject area, in relation to pupil needs and progress in the field, and in relationship to the total program within each school and within the district as a whole.

3. Selection of instructional materials to be used in implementing the curriculum, particularly text and supplementary books, supplies and equipment, and audio-visual and library or laboratory resources.

4. Improvement of instructional standards within the subject field, including in-service training of teachers to extend their mastery of their subject, selection of appropriate teaching methodologies, innovative practices in utilization of staff or facilities (including teaching teams and large and small group instruction), and related concerns such as class size policies.

5. Improvement of articulation of instruction among schools and among grade levels within the subject.

On the basis of his own experience serving on a district council such as that described above, the author predicts that few such councils will be able to accomplish all of their objectives in all of these areas during the course of a regular school year. Department heads in other subject fields confirm this experience: so much time at council meetings is necessarily given over to "business" items that there is little opportunity to engage in extended discussion of that most important question of all: "Why are we teaching what to whom?" That is, the agendas of most councils with which the author is familiar tend to focus very specifically on matters relating to item #3 above, the selection of instructional materials (books, athletic equipment, tools, paints, laboratory specimens, etc.) to be used in implementing the curriculum. As a result, the first item in any list of council responsibilities, definition and development of educational philosophies and curriculum, is often deferred to some future date "when there will be more time." Yet all of the practical and pressing decisions made during council sessions are really dependent on the educational philosophies of the council members.

This same situation usually prevails in the advisory councils of department heads who work with the principal and his administrative assistants in each individual school. Here, too, the immediate, the pressing, and the practical will always take precedence over questions which are abstract or long-range in nature.

The author is convinced that there is only one solution to this problem: the extended duty contract.

PROVIDING EXTENDED DUTY CONTRACTS

The extended duty contract provides time for department heads to meet and work together in their individual schools and in their district councils during a part of the summer vacation period, when they are free from the press of their classroom duties. It provides time for the kind of intensive, probing discussions of fundamental philosophies and practices that must precede sound educational planning. It is the only way in which a district can fully utilize the talents and experiences of its staff of department heads, and it is the key to giving truly professional, executive status to the department head position itself.

Extended duty contracts can be of two kinds. One, providing for approximately ten months of service, should be considered customary for every department headship. It requires department heads to be on duty in their schools or district for a week or two after the close of the regular session and to report for duty at least a week or two before the opening of the fall semester. This summer duty can be limited to half-day periods if a district wishes to keep its department chairmen available for participation in summer school teaching or in summer workshop programs. Limiting the period of required service to half-days during a part of the summer also enables chairmen to maintain their own professional growth by taking summer session courses at nearby colleges and universities.

The other kind of extended duty contract should be optional within a school or district. It offers an additional month of employment during the summer to department heads who present and have approved projects which will lead toward major improvements in existing instructional programs.

What should the chairmen do in their schools or district during the time provided by extended duty contracts? Obviously, administrators should not permit such contracts to become a means of subsidizing teacher clean-up or make-ready activities, where department heads work separately in their own rooms, putting away or getting out materials which they use in teaching their classes. Instead, administrators and chairmen must view this additional time as creating the opportunity for carrying on in-depth reviews of school and district programs and for engaging in conferences designed to improve the level of instructional and curricular leadership which department heads can provide.

At the local school level, administrators might establish the following general objectives for their department heads to meet during an extended duty period:

1. To undertake (or begin to undertake) a unified appraisal of the school's instructional programs, focusing upon curricula, personnel, resources, facilities, and organizational patterns,
2. To plan for the development of long-range activities leading toward the overall improvement of the school's instructional programs,
3. To establish guidelines for follow-up activities to be undertaken by teachers in each department, who will continue and refine the appraisal begun during the summer and then formulate specific departmental objectives designed to bring about desired improvements in the total school program.

These are challenging—indeed, formidable—objectives to set before any group! Yet administrators must recognize that anything less will leave a school's instructional programs fragmented and uncoordinated. There may continue to be changes and improvements in those programs, but they will be piecemeal and sporadic at best. A total school effort requires an assessment of the total school situation, undertaken by the united instructional leadership of that school.

How can administrators help their department heads meet these objectives? A logical first step is to establish a model of their programs of activities, displaying the various areas to be investigated and the procedures to be followed. This model might be more or less complex, depending upon the extent to which the staff is familiar with the principles and techniques of systems analysis. The chart on page 143 illustrates a simplified form of such a model.

To give a focus to their work, administrators should ask their department heads to evaluate the ability of their school's programs, personnel, facilities, and organizational structure to meet the needs of their students. For this purpose, a number of individuals from among those who attended the school recently must be contacted for follow-up information. Some of these should be graduates from the school who are now attending college or receiving training in an apprenticeship program of some kind. Some others should be married or in military service. And certainly some must be school or social drop-outs, not currently engaged in any sort of useful work. Through interviews and questionnaires, these former students could report the vocational and personal needs which they experienced after they left the school. The department head staff then evaluates the success of the school in providing these young adults with the skills and attitudes which they needed. From such an evaluation as this can emerge a school and district quality assurance program of major significance!

On a district level, some part of the time provided for department heads by extended duty contracts should be devoted to curriculum discussions with their colleagues in their district councils. Here they will compare the kinds of instructional programs which they have established in their individual departments and exchange ideas and information which are useful to each chairman as he plans ways to improve his performance during the coming year. Indeed, the same kind of creative analysis as that described above could be applied to an entire subject field within the district during the time made available to district councils for summer conferences.

An outstanding example of the kind of activities which can be conducted by school administrators and department heads during

AREAS AND TOPICS FOR POSSIBLE DISCUSSION
IN SCHOOL ASSESSMENT PROGRAM

Staff
Principal
Assistant Principals
Department Heads
Librarian
District Personnel (As appropriate)

Areas for Group Discussion

School Personnel	Programs
Selecting good teachers	Analyzing the curriculum in terms of
a. Interviewing techniques	student needs
b. Assigning and orienting	
	Developing interdisciplinary programs
Developing good teachers	
a. Effective supervision	Developing new resources and practices
b. Effective in-service training	a. Resource centers for individual study
c. Innovative staff utilization	b. Closed circuit TV
	c. Learner activity packages
Retaining good teachers	d. Differentiated class sizes
a. Encouraging creativity	e. Differentiated teacher roles
b. Proving rewards	
c. Solving problems	
ETC.	ETC.

School Facilities	School Organization
Achieving effective utilization of available facilities	Analyzing the effectiveness of the present school organizational structure
Planning desirable changes in present school facilities	Studying possibly desirable changes in the present organizational structure
a. Differentiated room sizes	a. Creation of interdisciplinary "task"
b. Resource centers	committees for particular types of
c. Development of outdoor learning facilities	students (basic, etc.) or particular types of skills (reading, composition, computation, etc.)
	b. Creation of departmental management committees
ETC.	ETC.

Formulation of plans and procedures for accomplishing improvements
Involvement of total school staff through faculty and departmental committees

143

a period of summer duty is the "Curriculum Associates Workshop" held in Redwood High School. This school, part of the Tamalpais Union High School District, is located just north of San Francisco.

The workshop lasted for two weeks during the summer of 1967. During this time, the administrative staff and curriculum associates (department heads) met daily for four hours. The objectives established for the workshop included the following:

1. To provide intensive in-service training for administrators and curriculum associates in the areas of organizational planning, curriculum innovation and development, teacher supervision, and departmental management.

2. To develop a specific program and time table for full implementation of new organizational planning for the school. This would include specific plans at the departmental level aimed at encouraging interdisciplinary curricular innovations.

3. To provide a springboard for the development of long-range plans and activities leading toward curricular improvement, new methodology, and new communications media.

Detailed selections from the *Report of Curriculum Associates Workshop,* prepared by the Redwood High School staff, appear in the appendix to this book. These selections indicate the scope of the workshop's activities and accomplishments. Included are the schedule of workshop activities, lists or resource persons and materials utilized, and specific accomplishments in improving the school's overall program, as well as the programs of several representative departments.

In general, the workshop's participating administrators and department heads reported that they had derived the following benefits from their summer round of conferences:

1. Administrators and curriculum associates gained a greater sense of the total problems of the school and of how their individual roles within the school could be of service in solving those problems.

2. The sharing of information contributed signifi-

cantly to a better understanding of the needs of each department in the school, in relation to the total school program.

3. Administrators and curriculum associates gained an appreciation of the value and the significance of each person's role in an integrated, school-wide program of instruction. The cirriculum associates and administrators became a more united group as a result of the workshop experience.

It is very difficult for the department heads and administrators of a school to find time during a regular academic year to engage in the kinds of discussion and activities listed in the report cited here. This is why the author recommends that districts make every effort to provide time during the summer vacation period for conferences of this nature to take place in their own schools. The instrument for accomplishing this is the extended duty contract. If it is not possible for a district to finance such contracts for all of its chairmen every year, it might still be possible to offer them to the department heads in each school in turn. This creates the opportunity for each school to engage in a program of evaluation and planning on a rotating basis, as its turn comes.

SUMMARY

Administrators who want to improve coordination and co-operation among department heads in their schools or district might do so with the recommendations presented in this chapter.

We saw how chairmen can meet and work together more effectively in their schools if their released periods are scheduled concurrently and if they convene from time to time in different teaching stations in each school.

We also saw how district councils should be structured so as to improve com—————————————————among the departments representing each subject area in a district's schools.

Finally, the case for providing department heads with extended duty contracts was presented, with a hypothetical and an actual example of how schools can use the time created by these contracts to achieve major evaluations and revisions of their total instructional programs.

9

Extending the Leadership of
Outstanding Department Heads

Among the department heads in any district will usually be found a few individuals with very marked talent for leadership. They are the district's acknowledged teacher-leaders, men and women whose abilities have won them recognition in their classrooms, promotion to department head positions, and then further distinction through their work in school and district programs. In their schools, their voices tend to carry the most weight in their principals' advisory councils. On the district level, they are most frequently elected to chair their subject area councils, and they are often consulted by school and district administrators on matters of policy relating to their fields.

But most districts do not begin to use the talents of these outstanding individuals as fully and effectively as they might. In an age when virtually every part of the educational scene is undergoing change at a revolutionary rate, the specialized training and experience of these master teacher-chairmen could provide hard-pressed administrators with invaluable assistance.

In this chapter, administrators will find some suggestions for making use of their own best department heads to improve the quality of educational leadership which they are able to provide in their schools and districts. They will see how these chairmen can enrich instructional programs by performing the following kinds of services:

1. **Research** Each year, administrators must make important and far-reaching decisions which affect total school programs. They must determine, for example, which "new English" or "new math" should be taught. They must select equipment for language laboratories or data processing classes which will provide the best opportunity for learning—and at the lowest purchase and maintenance costs. They must decide how indoor and outdoor facilities should be used in schools which adopt modular scheduling. If these decisions are based upon expert research, then correct choices most likely will be made, and districts will improve their instructional programs while avoiding costly mistakes. A district can use its best department heads to conduct this research in their areas of specialized knowledge and competency.

2. **Planning** Once research has been completed, plans can be prepared for making use of the information obtained. Goals and objectives can be established, and appropriate blocs of time can be assigned for meeting them. Alternative strategies can be devised for achieving these goals as quickly as district resources (particularly time, money, personnel, and facilities) permit. Here again, the top subject area leaders in a district can provide the specific information which plans require if they are to be feasible.

3. **Demonstration** As schools and districts move to implement plans, the most creative department heads can be used as consultants and demonstration teachers, to assist the general faculty in working toward the established goals and objectives.

In attempting to capitalize on the leadership potential of its most gifted department heads by assigning to them the roles just described, however, districts will likely encounter some very real and practical problems. During the regular school year, these chairmen are deeply involved in teaching their own classes and working with their departments and district councils. And even with the additional time provided by extended duty contracts (as recommended in the preceding chapter), they cannot free themselves sufficiently from their own regular assignments to exercise more general leadership within their districts.

The traditional and current practice in most districts is to provide staff with the time and relative freedom of operation which are required for the exercise of real leadership by promoting them to administrative positions. Many gifted department heads are reluctant to seek such promotions because they will be taken out of the very areas when they have been most successful in their work: the classroom and the department. They may also feel themselves unsuited for the many housekeeping and public relations duties which become the responsibility of the school administrator.

Thus, districts often find that they are unable to use their best department heads as fully as they should simply because there isn't enough time to be made available to them. And many chairmen have to accept the fact that they will play only limited roles in helping to improve district programs unless they are ready to enter the field of administration.

Is there a solution to this impasse? The author believes that there is.

What is required is the creation of a *limited* number of staff positions of an entirely new nature within a school or district, ranking somewhere between the level usually occupied by department heads and that assigned to vice-principals or similar administrative ranks. These positions should be created for outstanding department heads, to enable them to develop and apply their creativity, initiative, and general leadership abilities, without taking them entirely away from their classes and their departments. The following of such positions should be considered by a district which is seeking new ways to utilize the talents of its best subject area leaders. Such assignments allow for maximum development of the department head position in a school or district.

ESTABLISHING THE COORDINATING DEPARTMENT HEAD

The creation of this position does not constitute a very radical departure from staffing practices which are common to many high schools in the country. A coordinating department head performs many of the duties of a vice-principal for curriculum and instruction, a job appearing frequently in organizational charts for secondary schools. The author believes that a coordinating department head can perform those duties more effectively than the vice-principal, since the former is not removed from daily teaching responsibilities.

A coordinating department head is one of a school's existing staff of chairmen, selected by the principal (after consultation with the chairmen) to assume special responsibilities in addition to his regular assignment as a teacher and department head in the school. One of these responsibilities is to assist the principal in improving coordination of the school's instructional programs, perhaps by helping other chairmen to identify educational goals and objectives which are common to more than one subject field. Working with the principal, a coordinating department head then assists his colleagues in the task of creating instructional programs which will better integrate their efforts to reach those objectives. Thus, for example, an individual in such a position helps his colleagues to recognize that one of the English department's goals in teaching appreciation of a novel is closely related to the music department's purpose in teaching appreciation of a symphony, or the art department's goal in offering instruction in the principles of composition in painting. Acceptance of the implications of this kind of discovery can pave the way for the creation of an excellent inter-disciplinary humanities course in the school, where the unity of artistic vision and purpose is presented in a variety of forms, without regard to subject field boundaries.

In addition, a coordinating department head can be assigned by his principal to assist in the training and orientation of his fellow chairmen, particularly those newly-appointed to the position. Drawing on his own background of successful experiences as a chairman, the coordinator leads them in a study of effective practices in supervision, curriculum development, and departmental management. He might also be called in to assist a fellow chairman with a problem of teacher evaluation. Here, like the principal of his school, he utilizes his own knowledge of effective teaching techniques to supplement his colleague's more specialized background in the subject matter being covered in the classroom.

A department head who is to be promoted to this kind of coordinating position should meet the qualifications specified at the end of this chapter, to make certain that he will perform his duties effectively. In order to allow him to meet his additional responsibilities, he should receive at least one released period daily beyond those provided for his work in his own department. And finally, the author recommends that such a position carry with it an eleven-month contract, to provide the coordinator with the opportunity to work closely with administrative staffs on the school and district levels. Districts which wish to test this position can do so by establishing it first in one or two schools, where its usefulness in improving department head performance can be evaluated.

A position quite similar to that proposed here was established in the Sequoia Union High School District near San Francisco at the time when the author visited there during his study of the department headship. Each of the schools in that district supplemented its normal department head staff with one curriculum assistant, chosen by the school principal and the district assistant superintendent for instruction. Each curriculum assistant received two released periods daily in which to provide additional curriculum liaison within his school and between his school and the district's administration offices.

ESTABLISHING THE RESIDENT CURRICULUM ASSOCIATE

This is a much more innovative position than that of the coordinating department head just described. It offers the possibility of enlarging a chairman's area of leadership beyond the confines of the school to which he is regularly assigned. A resident curriculum associate becomes a district-wide teacher-leader; he serves as a resource, a guide, and an inspiration to all of the faculty, particularly in his subject area.

A resident curriculum associate is *the* outstanding teacher and department head in his field in the district, selected by his district council and confirmed by school and district administrators after careful consideration. He is released entirely from his regular classroom and departmental duties *during the year of his service in the position.* He should also be placed on an eleven-month contract and be supported by a salary equal to that of a school principal as well as by an adequate travel budget.

The position of resident curriculum associate resembles to some extent the position of subject area consultant or supervisor, which is often found in larger school districts. There are two important differences between their roles and functions, however.

For one, the resident curriculum associate works on the school level, moving from one school to another in his district as he carries out his assignment. Thus he is not considered a part of the district office staff. Secondly, the resident curriculum associate holds his position for only a limited period of time (probably not to exceed two years in even the largest districts). As soon as he has completed his circuit of the schools in his district, he leaves the position and returns to his regular assignment as a department head in one of those schools. The position of resident curriculum associate is then opened to an outstanding department head in a different subject area. He will also work in the district schools, but this time with the faculty in his field.

The author's district recently experimented with a position similar in many respects to that proposed here when it created a "district teacher of mathematics." The department head who occupied this post was a recognized authority in his field. Through this special assignment, he was able to share his knowledge and experience with mathematics teachers throughout the San Mateo Union High School District.

How does a resident curriculum associate serve a school or district? He is a master teacher-leader who is provided an opportunity to familiarize himself with the best practices in current use among teachers in his subject area. He gains this knowledge through research and travel. He then visits each school in his district in turn, serving for a period of time as a resident consultant in his subject area department. He brings to those departments an expert and objective viewpoint which enables him to undertake a thorough analysis of their instructional programs. After completing this analysis, he offers suggestions for improving the programs, the facilities in which they are being presented, and the staff and materials being used to implement them. In many cases, he is also able to participate directly in the programs, through joining in planning groups or offering the example of his own performance in demonstration teaching.

A job description for the specific duties and responsibilities of the position should include the following suggested items:

A SUGGESTED INITIAL JOB DESCRIPTION
FOR A RESIDENT CURRICULUM ASSOCIATE

1. The resident curriculum associate will be directly responsible to the assistant superintendents for instruction and personnel.

2. The resident curriculum associate will work closely with the principal and department head in each school to which he is assigned. He will clear all of his actions in advance with that principal and department head.

3. The resident curriculum associate will begin his term of office by visiting a number of outstanding schools in the state, selected by the superintendent's staff, and by making week-long "familiarization" visits to all of his subject area departments in his district.

4. The resident curriculum associate will serve in residence in as many of his district schools as possible, spending as many months at each as may be deemed appropriate by the superintendent's staff and the principal and department head concerned.

5. Working with the principal and the department head in his subject area in each school to which he is assigned, the resident curriculum associate will assume responsibilities in the following areas:

   A. **Improvement of Instruction**

      1. He may teach demonstration lessons or units, or team with teachers in his subject area department to demonstrate particular techniques of instruction or particular instructional materials, or to share his own background of subject matter information.

      2. He may assist the department head with the development and implementation of special instructional programs, including innovative practices in

        class sizes, teacher utilization, inter-disciplinary teaching, etc.

3. He will make himself available as a consultant to teachers in the department who wish special assistance in improving their teaching techniques or subject matter background.

B. **Curriculum Development**

1. He will examine the curriculum in the department and the materials and facilities which are available to implement it.

2. He will recommend to the principal and department head any changes which could improve the curriculum, the materials, or the facilities, being particularly alert for changes which can lead to increased inter-disciplinary planning and teaching.

3. He will serve as a communications link between schools in the district so that successful practices in his subject area in one school might be made known in all schools as quickly as possible.

4. He will attend all district council meetings in his subject area during the term of his appointment to this position. In addition, while he is in residence in a particular school, he will attend meetings of department heads and of teachers in his subject field in that school.

C. **Improvement of Articulation**

1. Soon after his arrival at a particular school in the district, he will visit the intermediate schools which "feed" into that school, to familiarize himself with the preparation which entering freshman students have received in his subject area. He will transmit this information to the principal and department head of the school to which he is assigned.

2. He will also familiarize himself with the freshman programs in his subject field in the major colleges and universities to which most of the district's graduates go. He may then assist the principal and department head in each school to which he is assigned to articulate their instructional program as closely as possible with those which their graduating seniors will be entering.

APPOINTING THE TEACHER EXECUTIVE

One of the most imaginative approaches to achieving maximum use of the talents of superior department heads in embodied in the teacher executive program established in the San Mateo Union High School District in California. This program was conceived by Dr. Leon M. Lessinger, then district superintendent and later Associate United States Commissioner for Elementary and Secondary Education, in the United States Office of Education. His plan provided an opportunity for outstanding department heads (and later, teachers) to leave their regular assignments for a year in order to carry out major projects for the district.

As the program was originally designed, department heads in the district were encouraged to apply for teacher executive positions. Those selected were assigned during the following school year to teach a full schedule of six classes daily, without any released time or preparation periods. However, intern teachers from nearby state colleges and universities were employed to work with the department heads in each class. During the first part of the school year, the chairmen worked very closely with their classes and intern assistants. As the weeks passed, they were gradually able to leave their classes under the direction of the intern teachers for longer and longer periods of time. Within a few months, the teacher executives were able to leave their classes entirely, returning only occasionally to supervise and confer with the assistant teachers. The teacher executives did continue to perform their regular department head duties, however.

Before examining the benefits derived by the district and the teacher executives themselves from the operation of this program, it might be interesting to point out one important feature of the plan as it operated initially: it was virtually self-supporting. It is true that the department heads chosen to serve as teacher executives received their full salaries, plus special increments of $1500 apiece, and the interns were also paid for their services. But by giving up their released periods to accept assignment to six classes daily, the chairmen enabled the district to achieve savings which met most of the expenses of the program. In effect, the teacher executive program enabled the district to provide good instruction in each of the teacher executives' classes, assist in the state's teacher training program, free a number of exceptionally talented department heads to engage in special projects, and receive the benefits from their work, all for the same expenditure that would have been required simply to support the chairmen in their regular capacities.

During the first year in which the teacher executive program was in operation in the San Mateo Union High School District, department heads who were selected for the position engaged in a wide variety of valuable, creative activities. Many of these would have been impossible for these individuals to undertake without the time and freedom provided by this innovative program. A sampling of reports prepared by the teacher executives gives an indication of the broad scope of their work. The following are representative of their activities:

1. *Curriculum development:* writing textbooks and establishing special student programs in their subject areas,

2. *Teacher training and staff utilization:* participating in team teaching and intern education programs,

3. *Teacher recruitment and selection:* attending conferences and interviewing teacher applicants in other parts of the country.

4. *Articulation:* meeting with the staffs of intermediate schools and local colleges to which district graduates apply,

5. *Visitation:* making local and national visits to model school programs or to study innovative practices in flexible scheduling, phased curricula, etc.,

6. *Demonstration teaching:* presenting guest lectures on topics of special interest before classes in most of the schools in the district.

But the question might be posed: what did these activities really accomplish by way of improving the district's instructional programs? What specific benefits were actually derived from the establishment and operation of the teacher executive plan? Administrators and teachers evaluated the program carefully after its first year and confirmed that it had proved its value in may ways:

1.   Students throughout the district had profited from the work of the teacher executives. Many had come into direct contact with these master teachers when they presented demonstration lessons and guest lectures in schools other than those in which they regularly served. Indeed, far from removing the teacher executive from the classroom, the program had actually made it possible for these chairmen to work directly with many more students than they normally did when they served in just one school. Furthermore, large numbers of other students had received the benefit of exposure to a variety of instructional materials prepared by the teacher executives but presented by their regular classroom teachers.

2.   The district's instructional programs were improved by the work of the teacher executives. Some of this improvement took place during the course of their year of service. Other changes were introduced later as the teacher executives brought to the district some of the programs and procedures which they had observed while visiting model schools in many parts of the country.

3.   Liaison between the district and other educational systems was greatly improved as a result of the program. Many contacts were made by the teacher executives which improved articulation between the schools in the district and neighboring elementary districts and colleges. Furthermore, the teacher executives had an opportunity to meet with outstanding administrators and teachers throughout the state and much of the nation as well. The exchange of information that developed from these conferences will benefit all of the systems concerned for years to come.

4.   The district made an important and mutually helpful contribution to teacher education programs

in nearby colleges and universities. Not only did the teacher executive plan provide interns with a chance to work closely with master teachers in a very desirable school setting, but it also afforded the district an opportunity to observe and train a very promising group of young instructors. Some of these individuals were offered regular contracts with the district at the conclusion of their internship.

5. Outstanding teachers were given a unique opportunity to improve themselves professionally and financially. It is rare for high school teachers to find situations in which they can travel or engage in research and experimentation while still employed on a full-time basis; these benefits are usually reserved for those who teach on the college or university level. The teacher executive program offered a selected group of outstanding department heads a unique experience which was richly satisfying and rewarding. It was an experience from which they and their district will continue to derive benefits for many years to come.

After its first year of operation, the teacher executive program underwent a number of procedural changes, in order to make it an even more valuable plan for the district and its faculty alike, and this evolution continues to the present writing.

As a first step, the program was opened to teachers as well as department heads, in order to draw on the creative talents of the entire staff of the district. A procedure was established whereby applicants for the position were screened and evaluated by the District Academy of Instruction (a faculty body composed of teachers elected from each school and representatives from each of the district's councils of department heads) and various administrative groups. In addition, the operational conditions of the position were altered: those named to become teacher executives were not assigned to any classroom or departmental duties at all during the year of their service in the position. Their classes were still taken by intern teachers, but the task of supervising these beginners was removed from the teacher executives and given to the heads of the departments in which they worked. In the event that the teacher executive was the regular department head (as was the author's case), an acting chairman was appointed for the year to release him from his departmental duties. As a result, the teacher executives were free to devote all of their time and efforts to the projects which they had proposed when applying for their positions.

Two teacher executives were appointed in the second year of the program. One developed a multi-media language arts program for use in reading laboratories. The other was the author, who prepared a series of recommendations for the improvement of department head policies and practices in his district. The number of appointees was necessarily small, however, because the teacher executive program was by this time no longer self-supporting. Instead, it now required a very considerable investment of district resources, for each teacher executive, drawing his full salary, an increment of $1000, and necessary travel funds, represented an expenditure of up to $16,000 in district money.

The author was one of those who became concerned about the limitations being placed on the program by its rising costs. It was quite clear that the district would be able to support only a few individuals in teacher executive positions each year, thus denying many talented teachers an opportunity to participate. Furthermore, the very fact that only a limited number could be chosen tended to favor applicants with large, district-wide projects, from which the maximum benefits could be derived. Consequently, many applicants with projects smaller in scope but extremely useful for one or two schools would tend to be passed over in the selection process.

District administrators and teachers (including the author) then designed new procedures for the teacher executive program, intended to open the position to more candidates, without increasing the cost borne by the district. In effect, these changes decentralized the teacher executive plan, to make it more responsive to the needs of particular schools and departments.

Under the new system of operation, the funds previously budgeted for salary increments and intern teacher salaries are applied instead to providing released time by hiring substitute teachers. These funds are allocated among the schools in the district, proportional to the size of their faculties. Department heads or full-time teachers who are interested in serving as teacher executives for short periods of time now submit their project applications to their individual school principals. Upon approval of the project, a specified number of days of released time is provided for the applicant, and he is freed to carry out his special assignment. Reports of accomplishments are required after the conclusion of each project, and results which have district-wide application are made available to all other schools in the district.

As may be seen from this summary, the teacher executive program offers a flexible, varied means of releasing talented staff members to engage in specialized, creative projects. It frees them for an entire year or for shorter periods of time. It replaces them with intern teachers or with substitute teachers. And the projects which are thus supported may lead to improvements in major, district-wide programs or in the operation of a single department within a single school.

On the basis of his personal experience in the teacher executive program, the author recommends it for careful consideration by districts which are seeking new ways in which to utilize the talents of their staffs, particularly of department heads, in order to improve the position.

SELECTING DEPARTMENT HEADS
FOR SPECIAL ASSIGNMENTS

Applicants for the position of coordinating department head, resident curriculum associate, or teacher executive should possess special abilities which qualify them for appointment. These qualifications will, of course, vary from district to district. The criteria listed below ought to be considered minimal.

Each applicant should demonstrate the following characteristics:

1. He has a well-developed philosophy of education which he implements capably in his professional activities;
2. He participates creatively in the professional activities of his teaching area;
3. He demonstrates outstanding subject matter com-

petency and shows himself able to contribute to new curricular and instructional developments;

4. He regularly experiments with new techniques and procedures in his department and classroom, and he reports his findings effectively to his colleagues;

5. He demonstrates his ability to play an active leadership role in his school and district;

6. He understands the total school program and is able to interpret it effectively to the community and to the faculty and students in the school;

7. He commands the respect of the community for his position and his achievements in the school system.

SUMMARY

This chapter has examined three programs which can enable a district to make maximum use of the talents of its most outstanding department heads.

These gifted teacher-leaders can make a major contribution to the improvement of a district's instructional programs by engaging in research, planning, and demonstration activities.

The coordinating department head, resident curriculum associate, and teacher executive programs offer a way to provide superior chairmen with the time and expanded field of operations that they require in order to engage in such activities. We saw how these three innovative plans work and how they benefit students and staff alike in a total school program. We also examined some of the essential qualifications which applicants for these positions should possess.

The innovative positions described in this chapter are not inexpensive—either in time or money. But they offer a channel for developing the full potentiality of the department headship for improving the instructional programs in a school or district.

10

Improving the Evaluation of Department Head Performance

Evaluation of actual performance is the essential final step in any district's program for improving the position of its department heads. Without such an appraisal, a school system cannot be certain that its efforts to improve the selection, training, and operations of its department heads have finally produced the desired result: superior performance.

And yet, in the many school districts which the author visited during the course of his study, there was little evidence that sound procedures had been established for regularly evaluating the work accomplished by department heads in their schools. For the most part, the evaluation that did take place was conducted by a single administrator (usually, the principal in each school or the district director of instruction). It typically consisted of subjective kinds of judgments, based on casual observations of department heads at work in their schools or in meetings at the district office. As might be expected, the results of such off-hand appraisals were often vague statements such as these:

"Well, he's doing a good job, all in all."

"He does seem to get along pretty well with most of his teachers."

"Anyway, *he* always gets his orders in on time!"

Obviously, it is difficult to determine the real strengths and weaknesses of any chairman's performance on the basis of such "evaluations" as those!

As an alternative, this chapter will outline plans for establishing a policy of *systematic,* annual evaluation of department head performance on a school or district level. We will also see that such evaluation can be carried on fairly and can produce objective and useful results if it involves administrators, teachers, and the department heads themselves in the process.

Before a workable system of evaluation can be proposed, however, three preliminary questions must be answered: what is to be measured, who is to do it, and by what procedures? Finding answers to these questions, as experienced administrators know, is not an easy matter.

The problem of trying to decide what is to be measured in order to obtain an index to the level of department head performance is closely related to the old problem of deciding what to measure as a means of determining meritorious teaching performance. Naturally enough, evaluators first seek objective, verifiable data to support their judgements, for subjective evaluations are always open to charges of being unfairly slanted. And yet, some kinds of objective data can be just as misleading when applied to measure the performance of a department head as when applied to measure the performance of a teacher:

> ". . . Department heads (must) be encouraged not to measure their achievements in terms of additional staff members secured, budget achieved, addition of new courses, establishment of required or prerequisite courses, number of students enrolled in their respective departments, and other quantifiable but unreliable measures of a department's worth to its school."[13]

Each of the above factors may be less a measure of successful department head performance than of a chairman's empire-building tendencies! Or they might simply point out his good fortune in having among his staff a number of outstanding teachers who attract large numbers of students to their courses. Indeed, factors such as mere numbers of courses added to a department's offerings might reflect nothing more than changes in graduation requirements which had been adopted by the state legislature or the district's board of trustees!

What must be measured is the individual performance of each department head. This is the ideal—can it be realized? Is it possible to focus on the actual day-to-day work of the chairman himself, on the actions which he performs while carrying out his assigned duties? A recent study suggests that such individual assessment *is* possible, at least in the area of the work done by the department head to improve instruction in his department.

The study was conducted under the chairmanship of Dr. Clarence Fielstra, professor of education at the University of California at Los Angeles.[14] The purpose of the work was to collect and analyze reports of department head behaviors which were directed toward providing services designed to improve instruction in their departments. Reports of these actions, both effective and ineffective in nature, were solicited from department heads and teachers in the secondary schools of Los Angeles; a total of 674 responses was utilized during the course of the study.

The key questions to be asked in an examination of the results of this project are whether it is possible for a department head and/or teacher to observe and report specific behavior on the part of the chairman, and, if so, whether it is also possible to judge the behavior so reported as being desirable or undesirable. According to Dr. Fielstra, a total of 1193 reports of behavior was collected by those making the study, and many of these reports repeated and reinforced each other. This indicated that it *was* possible for the respondents to observe and report behavior. Furthermore, it indicates that different respondents observed and reported the same kinds of behavior, thus lending validity to the observations. When the same actions are clearly apparent to different people and are present in their separate reports, then it may be said that such actions are objectively verifiable.

As to whether it is possible to judge the desirability or undesirability of the behaviors observed and reported, the conclusions to be derived from this study again seem to be affirmative. The author maintains that there can be little reasonable objection to the way in which Dr. Fielstra and his researchers evaluated the desirability of many of the actions reported. For example, among "effective behaviors" (each of which was reported by at least five respondents) are listed the following obviously desirable actions:

1. Gave demonstration lessons,
2. Showed a teacher how to reorganize class routines and reschedule daily programs,
3. Counseled a teacher on how to teach an unruly class,
4. Complimented the good work of the department,
5. Suggested sharing materials and equipment,
6. Worked with a teacher new to a subject,
7. Conferred with an observed teacher to discuss specific questions on teaching techniques,
8. Discussed curriculum guides and lesson plans with teachers,
9. Arranged for teachers to observe other classes; invited new teachers to observe his own classes,
10. Asked an experienced teacher to help a new teacher,
11. Encouraged teachers to develop ancillary course of study materials,
12. Helped teachers get the supplies that they needed,
13. Provided teaching materials and courses of study,
14. Asked teacher preferences before assigning classes; gave each teacher as many subject preferences as possible,
15. Assigned classes and conference periods fairly, democratically, and carefully.

It would be difficult to quarrel with the judgments expressed here and to assert that these were not "effective" (desirable) behaviors. Similarly, the author believes that many of the department head actions which were evaluated as being "ineffective" (undesirable) clearly merit that classification. Consider, for example, the following actions (each reported by at least five respondents) which were labeled "ineffective":

1. Offered no suggestions concerning teaching methods, curriculum, or courses of study,
2. Was discourteous to speakers,

3. Failed to counsel or communicate with a new teacher,
4. Insisted that only one teaching system was acceptable,
5. Gossiped and violated teacher confidence,
6. Did nothing about the uniform marking system suggested by department members,
7. Kept the stockroom poorly organized; refused teachers access to equipment and supplies,
8. Made the master program without consulting department members,
9. Assigned classes on the basis of favoritism; refused to let a teacher teach his specialty,
10. Did not volunteer to assume his fair share of the load of class substitutions.

On the basis of this study, Dr. Fielstra reported that the following conclusions were reached:

"1. The overt, supervisory behaviors of department heads in secondary schools were observable, qualitatively distinguishable, and reportable to a third party by department heads and teachers.

"2. All department head behaviors reported by department heads were also reported by teachers. It thus appears that all overt department head behaviors were visible to the teachers they serve.

"3. The department head's actions as a leader of the group—actions he took to maintain organization communication, secure services from individuals, and formulate purposes and objectives—were observed and reported significantly more often than his actions as manager and scheduler...

"4. Department head supervisory actions involving inservice education activities, such as holding department meetings, organization of workshops, visitation of classes, and advice on curricular matters, were reported more often than were actions involving managing or scheduling.

"5. Teachers and department heads between the ages

of 21 and 40 reported generally the same kind of
department head behaviors as did teachers and
department heads between the ages of 41 and 65.
It appears that the services of department heads
were needed for teachers of all ages, and that the
kind of services needed did not change greatly as
the teachers got older.

"6. Department heads were frequently seen to behave
as curriculum leaders. The ineffective behaviors
reported did not always seem to indicate a lack of
knowledge of subject matter on the part of the
department head. Often, the department head's
lack of group or individual communication skill
appeared to prevent him from sharing the knowledge he had.

"7. Almost without exception, effective supervisory
actions observed by teachers and department heads
were those which required abilities beyond those
usually expected of the classroom teacher, especially in the areas of human relations, group leadership, and knowledge of the curriculum."[15]

This study has been quoted at length because, in the author's
opinion, it offers the essential answers to the three questions
posed at the beginning of this chapter: what is to be evaluated, by
whom, and how?

To the first question, the study directed by Dr. Fielstra
confirms the author's belief that effective evaluation can and
should be a measurement of the actual performance of department
heads. The findings of the study indicate that individual assessment of each chairman's actions is possible and that the results of
the assessment will be objectively verifiable. Further, the author
believes that the job description established in a district for its
department heads provides a suitable reference point for determining what should be measured, in order to evaluate their
performance. A job description indicates the kinds of actions that
are expected of a chairman; evaluation then becomes a matter of
determining whether these actions have been carried out effectively.

To the second question, the study shows that the evaluation can be conducted by personnel at more than one level in a school or district. The reports cited in the study came from two sources: the department heads themselves and their teachers. To this the author recommends adding a third source: the school principal. A possible fourth evaluator can be a district-level administrator such as an assistant superintendent for instruction or a director of personnel. Evaluation which is based on such multi-level observation and reporting cannot easily be called slanted or incomplete.

As for the procedures by which evaluation should take place, in the following pages the author will suggest some detailed steps which schools and districts might take. These will provide a systematic means of annually evaluating the performance of department heads, the critical link in completing any program designed to improve the department head position.

EVALUATING THROUGH TEACHER REPORTS

The evaluation process might logically begin with rating sheets filled out by the teachers in each chairman's department. These teachers should be provided with copies of the district's job description for department heads when they prepare the evaluations, so that they will understand the specific responsibilities which have been assigned to their chairmen. They can then judge how effectively their chairman's actions have met these responsibilities.

Should the evaluation forms be signed? A case can be made that unsigned ratings constitute a kind of secret trial before bidden accusers. On the other hand, however, an honest evaluation with signature attached can place a teacher's assignments or tenure in jeopardy because of reprisals from an unscrupulous tyrant of a chairman. Again, a case can be made that secret evaluation forms offer a disgruntled teacher the opportunity to attack his department head unfairly. In such cases, however, it can be expected that these attacks will be balanced by more objective reports from other teachers in the department. Furthermore, even an unjustly slanted evaluation signals the presence of a problem within the department (even if the problem represents only a communications failure between the chairman and a particular teacher) which should receive the prompt attention of the department head.

The author believes that evaluation forms should *not* be signed if copies are given directly to the chairman concerned. If the forms are signed, then each chairman should receive only a summary report prepared by the principal, representing a composite of the ratings from the individual teachers in his department. Furthermore, the entire evaluation process should be personally supervised by the principal or another administrative officer from the school, so that it will be perceived by the entire faculty as a serious exercise of professional responsibility on the part of all concerned.

The actual rating instrument itself can take any of several possible forms. It can be just a check sheet, with a list of department head duties and a series of blanks in which the appropriate check is placed, to indicate how well the duties are performed. Or, it can be a combination check sheet and anecdotal report. In this kind of form, which the author recommends, the chairman's overall accomplishments in certain major areas of responsibility (such as curricular leadership, instructional leadership, staff relationships, and departmental management) are rated by a check, but these evaluations are supported and illustrated by reports of specific actions which the chairman has performed and his teachers have observed.

A model for such a combined rating and report sheet by which teachers in a department can evaluate their chairman's performance appears on page 169.

EVALUATING THROUGH DEPARTMENT HEAD REPORTS

The second instrument recommended for department head evaluation is a report prepared annually by each chairman. The chairman's report reviews what his department has accomplished that year toward improving its instructional programs and what it has contributed to the improvement of the total school program (such as in the area of achieving better coordination with the work of other departments). It also indicates what part the chairman personally and individually played in exercising leadership to accomplish those improvements. Finally, the report contains the

A SUGGESTED INSTRUMENT FOR TEACHER EVALUATION
OF DEPARTMENT HEAD PERFORMANCE

Department Head: _____ Date: _____

School: _____ Department:_____

Enter a check mark in the column which best describes the level of your department head's performance in each area. The columns are marked G for GOOD, S for SATISFACTORY, and U for UNSATISFACTORY. Use the spaces under each area for comments to support your rating. Use the back of the sheet for further comments if you wish.

G   S   U

_   _   _   CURRICULAR LEADERSHIP (providing leadership in curriculum development; assisting teachers with current developments in their subject area; encouraging exchanges of ideas within the department; conducting worthwhile meetings; effectively representing the department in the school or district)

_   _   _   INSTRUCTIONAL LEADERSHIP (evaluating teachers fairly and constructively; giving teachers instructional aid through observations and conferences; encouraging teachers to develop their own skills; effectively utilizing teachers' strengths and interests within the department and school)

_   _   _   STAFF RELATIONSHIPS (recognizing teachers' individuality; treating teachers professionally; developing and maintaining the respect and confidence of teachers in the department)

_   _   _   DEPARTMENTAL MANAGEMENT (efficiently managing departmental supplies, materials, and facilities; providing instructional resources for teachers; efficiently discharging responsibilities in areas of departmental budget, correspondence, etc.)

department head's perceptions of major problems or opportunities still ahead for his department or for the school as a whole, and his suggestions for ways of dealing with them. A review of this nature should probably be prepared in narrative form; a simple check list might be too generalized to be very useful for such a report.

A thorough review such as this can be valuable to a school system for a number of reasons. It gives, of course, one important index of the effectiveness of a department head's performance. Furthermore, by allowing the chairman to "tell his side of the story," the report helps to provide objectivity and balance to the evaluations prepared by the teachers in his department. Beyond this, such reports provide administrators with very useful information about the "state of the union" within a school. This information can help alert them to problems or opportunities with which they should be concerned.

EVALUATING THROUGH ADMINISTRATIVE REPORTS

As a final step in the evaluation process, each chairman's performance should be judged annually by his principal and/or an administrator from the district's central office. This provides the essential third level of evaluation, from the perspective of an educator whose responsibilities extend beyond the individual classroom or department.

The administrative evaluation form probably should combine a check list with narrative comments to support the ratings given. The actual content of the form can be one of two kinds. The first allows for a general assessment of a department head's overall performance as a leader in his subject area. The specific items in such a form should be taken from the district's job description for department heads, in which case the administrative report will resemble to some degree the rating form used by the teachers in each chairman's department. The other kind of instrument evaluates the department head's success in meeting instructional objectives previously established within the district and school. An evaluation of this nature reflects the application of systems analysis techniques to the field of education, for it "closes the loop" and supplies the feedback information which is an essential element in the systems approach. Such a system could operate in a school district in the following manner:

Initially, school and district level administrators meet to study the annual reports prepared by their department heads, to determine some of the major instructional needs existing in the district. For illustration, the reports might indicate that a problem exists in all of the curricula designed for average or below-average students, in that the needs of these students are not being met as effectively as are the needs of college-bound pupils. Other reports might show that specific weaknesses exist in the district's adaptive physical education programs or in reading improvement classes and that corrective measures are required to bring achievement in these areas up to desired standards. Of course, department head reports will not be the only source of information about the district's instructional needs. Classroom teachers, members of the faculty serving on special assignments (such as those named to be resident curriculum associates or teacher executives), and the administrators themselves will all provide information and recommendations concerning the district's instructional programs.

The needs thus identified can then guide school and district administrators in the task of formulating broad annual and on-going educational objectives for all subject areas. By the determiniation of these objectives, the district commits itself to give top priority in financial and other support for programs designed to meet these goals.

The broad objectives thus determined for a district are then refined at the individual school level in conferences and planning sessions involving the superintendent, his staff, and the school principals. Similarly, a school's goals are translated into specific objectives for each department in conferences between the principal and his department heads. These mutually-determined goals provide guidelines for a good share of each department's activities during the school year.

At the end of each year, principals then evaluate their chairmen on the basis of their achievements in meeting the goals established for their departments. In some cases, the objectives will all have been met, and this offers one measure of the effectiveness of the leadership exercised by the department head. In other instances, the goals will have been met only in part, or even not at all. When this is the case, the principal confers with the department head involved to determine the cause for this "failure." They might decide that the objectives had not been realistic in the first place; this could serve as a valuable learning experience for administrator and chairman alike. Sometimes, unforeseeable circumstances will prevent a department from achieving its instructional objectives. On the other hand, unwarranted or unexplainable failure to meet the goals set for the department can indicate a defeciency in the performance of that department head.

FOLLOWING-UP THE EVALUATIONS

What should be done with the evaluations prepared by the teachers in a department, the department head himself, and school or district administrators?

The author recommends that one copy of each should go to the department head concerned, for his information and guidance. Evaluations prepared by a chairman's colleagues and administrative superiors will give him very valuable insight into the effectiveness of his performance, at least as it is perceived by those working most closely with him. This insight helps a good, conscientious department head take steps to improve his work by correcting whatever weaknesses have been identified. A second copy of each evaluation should be retained by the school principal. These evaluation reports should form an important part of his personnel files, to be consulted each year, at the time when department head appointments are recommended. And finally, at least one additional copy of each evaluation should go to an appropriate district level administrator, perhaps to a director of instruction or director of personnel. From these reports, the central office staff gains a better understanding of the instructional programs being presented in the district schools, as well as a clear evaluation of the effectiveness of some of the key people responsible for implementing those programs: the department heads.

In the event that a department head's performance receives an unfavorable evaluation through one or more of the instruments proposed here, the chairman and his principal (and perhaps a member of the superintendent's staff as well) should meet to review the situation carefully and thoroughly. Where necessary, they should work together to design a program for in-service training, by means of which the chairman will have an opportunity to improve his performance. Department heads who are unwilling or unable to upgrade their work sufficiently within a specified, reasonable period of time must, of course, be replaced in their positions at the earliest opportunity.

Whenever it becomes necessary to replace a department head, whether through his own choice or by administrative decision, the vacancy thus created should be announced throughout the district. At that point, the procedures for selecting and training new department heads recommended earlier in this book should go into effect, and the cycle begins anew.

SUMMARY

Evaluation of a chairman's actual performance on the job is the final step in any district program designed to produce effective school department heads. This chapter has reviewed a study conducted in Los Angeles which demonstrates that it is possible to conduct such evaluations objectively and to involve both teachers and department heads in the process. A program for carrying out multi-level evaluations of department head performance was then outlined. This program calls for chairmen to be judged by their teachers, through their own reports, and by their administrative superiors. Finally, recommendations were made for the effective use of these evaluation instruments, particularly where the need for improvement in a department head's performance is indicated.

11

Defining
the Department Head Position
in the Schools of Tomorrow

All of the preceding chapters in this book have examined the work and the position of the school department head *as he exists in the typical school situation of today.*

The author's purpose in Part One of this book was to suggest ways in which administrators can evaluate how effectively their chairmen meet their current responsibilities in the areas of teacher selection and supervision, curriculum development, instructional leadership, and departmental management. The author then proposed a series of steps which administrators can take to help their chairmen improve their work in each of these areas, when the evaluations indicated that the chairmen are not carrying out their duties effectively.

Part Two of this book has offered a program of specific recommendations for improving the framework in which department heads now operate. As we have seen, these proposals affect the selection, training, operational conditions, and evaluation of department heads. Again, this program of recommendations is designed for chairmen who are working in the typical school of today.

174

At this point, the question might logically and fairly be put: what of the department head in the schools of tomorrow? What will his situation be like? Will the role and functions of the chairmen working in the schools of 1990 be radically different from those of the chairman of today? If so, then the recommendations presented thus far in this book may have only short-term value.

How can this question be answered? What reasonable predictions can we make concerning the school department head of the future? The answer lies, in the author's opinion, in the successes and failures which have resulted from a number of experiments tried in recent years.

Within the past decade, the department head position has been the subject of a great deal of discussion and experimentation in schools of education and school districts alike throughout the country. (The author's teacher executive project—and this book—are cases in point.) The goal in every instance has been to find ways in which to improve the effectiveness of the chairman's work as an instructional and curricular leader within his school. As a result of some of these efforts, the department head position has undergone significant changes in a number of school districts.

The most common of these changes has been an expansion of the area of responsibility and influence assigned to the chairman. In many instances, this growth in the importance of the chairman's position has been accompanied by a change in title ("curriculum associate" and "division head" being the two most frequently reported) and a corresponding increase in the amount of released time and the size of the salary increment provided for the office.

Have these innovations produced the improvement in department head performance that was anticipated? Administrators who are concerned with upgrading the work of their own chairmen need to know what experiments have been proposed and what results have been achieved. In this chapter, we will examine in detail a representative selection of the changes that have been tested, to determine whether they point the way toward the department headship of the future.

The conclusions which will be reached concerning the value of the new approaches to providing subject area leadership are based on the author's own first-hand observations as well as on the evidence published in a number of research studies. The author personally studied some of the new plans in operation when he visited school districts in the San Francisco and Los Angeles areas during the course of his teacher executive project. During these visits, he had an opportunity to talk with administrators and teachers in those systems, to get their frank evaluations of the strengths and weaknesses inherent in the new roles being assigned to their subject area leaders. Similar judgments have also been expressed in dozens of articles appearing in the literature of the profession in recent years. These articles have published the findings of major research studies which were conducted to test the effectiveness of some of the new organizational structures.

One of these new plans was put into operation at Berkeley High School in California—with quite unexpected results.

EVALUATING A PLAN FOR
DISTRICT-SCHOOL COORDINATORS

Until a few years ago, the Berkeley Unified School District employed a staff of subject area specialists who operated out of the district office as consultants and supervisors. In addition, there were department head positions established at Berkeley High School, a comprehensive metropolitan school with a large and diversified student population. Some, but not all of these department heads were provided with released time for carrying out their duties.

With the coming of a new superintendent to the district, the supervisor positions were eliminated. At the same time, the high school department heads were given greater areas of responsibility, to provide a new kind of school-district leadership service. The department heads were now designated "curriculum associates" and were given dual assignments. They continued to serve as heads of their respective subject area departments within the high school. In addition, they were made responsible for coordinating curriculum and improving instruction in their fields in the district's junior high schools, so as to improve articulation between the programs on the junior and senior high school levels. This additional responsibility took them directly into the district's intermediate schools, where they worked closely with the principals and subject area chairmen in those buildings. In order to make it possible for the curriculum associates to meet their new responsibilities, they were given reduced teaching assignments in the high school; in some cases, they taught only a single class each day. They were also given salary increments which ranged substantially above the teachers' salary schedule established for the district. In 1968, these increments varied from $1090 to $1635 above the salary provided by their positions on the district schedule.

An examination of the job description drawn up for the curriculum associates (immediately following this section) shows that they provided all of the services for their departments which are typically provided by department heads who work entirely on their high school campuses. Their expanded responsibilities, however, tended to take them away from the high school a good deal of the time, particularly while they were serving as supervisors, curriculum consultants, and general "trouble-shooters" in the junior high schools.

Within two years after the new organizational plan went into effect, it became apparent that the curriculum associates were carrying such heavy loads of extended responsibility that they were no longer able to provide adequate leadership within their own departments in the high school. Interestingly enough, it was the teachers of Berkeley High School who first pointed out this fact. They petitioned the district administration to re-establish separate department head positions at the high school, to be staffed by teacher-leaders who would work *only* on that campus and who would be responsible *only* for meeting the needs of the faculty there. This request was granted, and chairmen were appointed for each department, to take over many of the customary duties of the chairman within each area (see the job description which foilows). Department chairmen were also given reduced teaching loads and substantial salary increments (ranging form $400 to $600 in 1968) for their added responsibilities.

An important conclusion can be drawn from this sequence of events. In this district at least—and there is no reason to believe that this in an a typical situation—there was demonstrated a clear need for subject area department heads who would work directly and entirely within the high school. The attempt to expand the department head position in such a way as to enable the chairmen to leave their school and operate on a district-wide basis created a vacuum within the high school which was recognized by teachers as well as administrators. And so necessary was it to fill that vacuum and to restore the services provided by their department heads, that the teachers themselves initiated the action which led to the re-creation of separate department head positions. A conclusion concerning the value and importance of the work carried on by the subject area department head seems obvious on the basis of the unexpected developments at Berkeley.

Whether the Berkeley system's present experiment in providing a kind of dual leadership by the curriculum associates and the department heads will work effectively in the future remains to be seen. When the author visited the school, to talk with administrators, curriculum associates, department chairmen and teachers, he heard frequent expressions of concern that the curriculum associates might eventually evolve into the same kind of district level supervisors whom they themselves had originally replaced. No such concern was expressed over the future of the department chairmen's position, however. The need for the leadership provided by the individual department chairmen has been clearly established, for the future as well as for the present.

BERKELEY UNIFIED SCHOOL DISTRICT
RESPONSIBILITIES OF CURRICULUM ASSOCIATES*

The major role of the Curriculum Associate is outlined below, but the functions and duties will vary with the various subject areas and with the size and complexities of the department.

    I.   Position of Curriculum Associate Within the Framework of Organization.

        A.   Each Curriculum Associate teaches one or more periods per day and as a teacher, he is directly responsible to his principal.

        B.   The Curriculum Associate will have the administrative responsibility for the operation of the department in

*Reprinted by permission of the Berkeley Unified School District

the school to which he is assigned. When the size and complexity of a department are such that one person cannot adequately perform the duties there shall be a Department Chairman in addition to the Curriculum Associate in that department. The Curriculum Associate will be directly responsible to the principal of each secondary school in administrative affairs and to the Director of Secondary Education in curriculum planning and development. He will be responsible for keeping the principals of the various schools informed on all curricular matters.

C. The Curriculum Associate will not be given study hall assignments or other assignments not clearly related to his work, unless special circumstances make this clearly desirable.

D. If the Curriculum Associate performs the duties of the Department Chairman in the school where he teaches, he is responsible directly to the principal.

E. In matters not related to the school in which he teaches, he is responsible to the Director of Secondary Education.

F. When working with Department Chairmen and with teachers in schools other than his own, the Curriculum Associate should clear all matters affecting that school with the respective principal.

II. Coordination and Articulation

A. The Curriculum Associate is responsible for the logical and systematic sequence in course content for grades 7 through 12. In some areas, such as Performing Arts, this responsibility extends to the elementary grades as well.

B. He will work with the elementary consultant in his field to secure articulation between the elementary and secondary schools.

C. He will represent the views of his field of instruction or coordination to the administration, the Board, and the community.

III. Curriculum Study and Development

A. The Curriculum Associate will help teachers to keep abreast of new developments in his field; this may be done through district-wide department meetings, discussions, bulletins and suggested readings.

B.   He will establish, together with the Department Chairmen, curriculum committees in each subject area and will make sure that there is a regular evaluation of the content of courses.

C.   He will see that minor changes in the curriculum are made when necessary and will refer suggested major changes to the principal and the Director of Secondary Education. He will supervise the work of course revision and the development of new courses.

D.   He will establish and maintain a systematic testing program; this need not be frequent, but it should be done in subject areas where it is practicable.

E.   He will keep abreast of the textbook revisions and new publications and make recommendations for new adoptions when these are desirable.

F.   He will investigate possibilities, develop projects and make applications, with the help of the Department Chairmen, for Federal, State and other educational aid programs.

IV.   Improvement in Instruction
To help bring about improvement in instruction the Curriculum Associate will:

A.   Observe classroom teaching.

B.   Participate in the evaluation of probationary teachers in all secondary school; written evaluations will be prepared.

C.   Review and aid in the development of lesson plans and study guides or courses of study.

D.   Arrange for some of the in-service training for new teachers in order that they may adjust more readily to their schools.

E.   Advise and assist in the selection and placement of new teachers.

RESPONSIBILITIES OF DEPARTMENT CHAIRMEN

In each secondary school there will be a Department Chairman, or a Curriculum Associate in charge of the department. The scope of the position of Department Chairman varies somewhat with the size and complexity of the department. Where the departments are large or complex, there will be a

Department Chairman. Where the departments are not large or complex, the principal will decide the need for a Department Chairman. Where a Department Chairman is not needed, and a Curriculum Associate is not assigned to the school, a representative to meetings of Curriculum Associates and/or Department Chairmen should be designated by the principal.

Each Department Chairman and department representative is directly responsible:

a) To the Curriculum Associate in all matters pertaining to curriculum planning and development,

b) To the principal of his school in other matters, except that if there is a Curriculum Associate at the school, the Department Chairman is responsible to the Curriculum Associate for matters pertaining to curriculum implementation.

The major functions of the Department Chairman are outlined below:

I.   Teaching
    A.   The size and complexity of the department will determine the amount of time released from classroom duties.
    B.   The Department Chairman will not be given study hall assignments or other assignments not clearly related to his work as a Department Chairman unless special circumstance makes this necessary.

II. Planning and Budget
    The Department Chairman will:

    A.   Prepare budget requests with the assistance of teachers in his department.
    B.   Assemble information necessary to order books, supplies and equipment and make certain that all things ordered are received.
    C.   Assist in making and adjusting the school's master schedule.
    D.   Be responsible for arranging for the maintenance, repair and inventory of department equipment.
    E.   Be a member of the school's budget committee.
    F.   Assist the Curriculum Associate in the investigation of possibilities, development of projects, and the making of applications for Federal, State, and other educational aid programs.

III. Improvement of Instruction
    The Department Chairman will:

A. Observe classroom teaching as time permits with special attention to beginning teachers. The purpose will be to give guidance and assistance.

B. Participate in the rating of probationary teachers within the department; written evaluations will be prepared.

C. Assist teachers in the handling of discipline problems which are related to teaching.

D. Conduct department meetings; these should normally be planned in consultation with the Curriculum Associate unless for the purpose of meeting purely local school problems.

E. Interpret the department's requirements to counselors and students.

F. Assist the Curriculum Associate and teachers in the department in developing curriculum and providing for curriculum continuity between all levels of education.

G. Assist when possible in the interview of prospective staff members.

EVALUATING A PLAN FOR SCHOOL COORDINATORS

The new organizational plan established in the Whittier Union High School District, in a suburb of Los Angeles, appears to offer all of the benefits possible in the Berkeley experiment while avoiding its drawbacks.[16]

In the Whittier district, a kind of expanded department head position was also developed, resembling the curriculum associates at Berkeley High School. But these "curriculum coordinators" worked entirely within their own high schools and had no responsibilities in the area's intermediate schools. As in Berkeley, each subject area department in Whittier's high schools had its own chairman. These chairmen did not receive any released time for carrying out their duties, however. The Whittier district, in effect, retained its departmental structure, with a subject matter specialist heading each department, but concentrated the released time that once was apportioned to the separate chairmen into full-time coordinating positions in each school.

The basic premise underlying the Whittier plan was that master teachers who are given sufficient time can make significant contributions toward the improvement of instruction in their schools. The curriculum coordinators in that district were just such master teachers. They had each been recommended for their teaching proficiency, had established records of leadership in professional organizations, and held masters degrees and appropriate teaching and administrative credentials. The coordinators provided leadership and direction in the development of curriculum and instructional materials. They also visited classes and assisted their school administrators with teacher evaluation, although the coordinators were primarily considered staff rather than line personnel.

Each curriculum coordinator was released full-time from classroom teaching responsibilities; in addition, he received a six percent salary differential above the regular teachers' salary schedule. Working closely with the coordinators were the individual department chairmen, who received salary increments of three percent but who were not provided with released time.

As the Whittier plan was originally conceived, there were to have been three full-time curriculum coordinators in each high school: one in English and social studies; one in foreign languages, science, and mathematics; and one in art, music, business, and industrial arts. Subsequent budgetary limitations required that the number be reduced, however, and at the time of the author's visit to the district, there was just one curriculum coordinator on duty in each school, with responsibilities in all the curricular areas specified above.

What benefits might be anticipated from adoption of the organizational plan now established in the Whittier Union High School District?

As indicated in the position analysis which follows, the curriculum coordinator is in a position to undertake quite extensive projects leading toward improvement of instruction and development of inter-disciplinary teaching programs. He has the time to work for as long as may be necessary with individual teachers who require assistance in improving their work, or with groups of department chairmen who are to be involved in experiments designed to up-grade the quality of the teaching performed by their staffs.

When the author visited the Whittier district during the course of his study of the department head position, to find out what the curriculum coordinator plan had actually achieved, he found the work of the individuals appointed to the position consistently praised by the administrators with whom he met. The district superintendent, for example, cited the fact that the facilities of the district's foreign language laboratories were being used by both English and foreign language teachers as one step toward curriculum coordination achieved through the efforts of the coordinators. He also pointed out that many of the instructional materials developed by the coordinators were being used in classes in a variety of subject fields, another instance of how the work of the curriculum coordinators crosses departmental lines.

Another benefit afforded by the Whittier plan stems from the fact that the curriculum coordinator's position formed a key intermediate step between department chairman and principal in the district's "promotion ladder." As has been noted before in this book, the typical practice in most districts is to promote good teachers away from *primary* involvement with curriculum and instruction after they rise above the department head level. Before a department head can become a principal in most school systems, he must rise through administrative posts whose immediate concern is with student conduct, guidance, activities, or the school budget. By contrast, the Whittier district's promotion path led from department chairman to curriculum coordinator, then to assistant principal for instruction, and then to the school principalship itself. Thus, at each step of his career, the would-be principal in that district was directly involved with the schools' major concerns: curriculum and instruction. This might be a point worth considering in districts which are seeking ways to retain their best teaching personnel in positions which deal directly with good classroom teaching, in order to avoid the not-uncommon practice of promoting a good teacher into a position for whose duties he might be unsuited.

In the final analysis, however, the success of the curriculum coordinator plan in the Whittier Union High School District depended on the ability of the coordinators to involve themselves effectively throughout their school. The real test of the plan was the effectiveness of the coordinators in supervising instruction and developing curriculum in all of the many subjects offered in the comprehensive high school.

In the author's judgment, based upon his discussions with principals, curriculum coordinators, and district level administrators at Whittier, the curriculum coordinators were in fact not very closely involved with the details of everyday instruction in their schools but rather were used as "floating trouble-shooters" (in the words of one of the coordinators) to take care of special problems. Meanwhile, the real task of providing classroom teachers with continuous, detailed assistance in choosing, organizing, and presenting their instructional programs seemed to fall to the individual department chairmen. A study of the job description created for the chairmen in that district confirms that such work does remain a major part of the department chairman's assignment in that system, despite the presence of the full-time curriculum coordinators assigned to each school.

WHITTIER UNION HIGH SCHOOL DISTRICT*
Duties of Curriculum Coordinators
1. The coordinators of instruction have the delegated responsibility for the coordination of the various curricular offerings within specific departments.
2. They supervise instruction within those areas.
3. They assist with the in-service training program and with the orientation of new teachers.
4. They work with department chairmen and teachers in the improvement of instruction and coordinate the preparation and administration of budgets in their assigned areas.
5. They act as consultants and resource persons in the preparation of materials and the use of methods and teaching techniques.
6. They assist the assistant principal in liaison and communication between teachers and the district office in emergency matters.
7. They assist teachers in arranging for field trips.

*Reprinted by permission of the Whittier Union High School District.

8. They assist teachers, at the direction of the assistant principal, who are having instructional problems.
9. They assist in the area of control and utilization of materials on the local campus.

Typical Responsibilities of Curriculum Coordinators

1. Coordination of textbook distribution and supply.
2. Follow-up on arrangements for special speakers, programs, field trips, etc.
3. Coordination of inventory control and scheduling of interdepartmental equipment and materials.
4. Coordination of budget ordering of books, supplies, and materials.
5. Coordination and follow-up on in-service training needs of teachers.
6. Coordination and implementation of curriculum development plans.
7. Coordination and recording of evaluation materials.
8. Consultant on teacher assignment and scheduling.
9. Staff liaison between administration and teachers.
10. Classroom visitation and supervision of instruction.
11. Consultant for visiting teachers and other dignitaries.
12. Methods and pedagogical techniques specialist for teachers.
13. Professional consultant to teachers on all problems.
14. Be a master teacher, with all its implications.

Department Chairman Responsibilities

(Monte Vista High School, Whittier Union High School District)

1. Provide leadership for the department in the areas of curriculum development and instruction as a master teacher.
   a. Assist teachers with the development of instructional units, tests, and course outlines, as necessary or requested.
   b. Assist with the supervision of the curriculum and instructional methods used by the department or its members.
2. Assist with the implementation of the department in-service training program.
   a. Provide the opportunity for department classroom visitations for the purpose of exchange of ideas.
   b. Assist with the organization of department in-service sessions which utilize district and/or outside resource personnel.

3. Act as a liaison person for the purpose of two-way communication between the various offices and members of the departments.
4. Supervise the use of equipment, materials, and supplies.
5. Assist with the preparation of the budget.
6. Assist with the coordination and development of the department film schedule.
7. Assist with the integration of the department's program into the total curriculum.
8. Participate in the work of the district curriculum study groups.
9. Other duties as assigned by the principal.

SUMMING UP THE CALIFORNIA EXPERIMENTS

At the opening of this chapter, we posed a critically important question: what will be the role and functions of the department head in the school of the future? Thus far, we have examined the plans which were put into effect in two California school districts, plans designed to create an expanded department head position in the schools of those districts. Do these experiments point the way to the effective school "department head" of tomorrow? To answer this, we must determine what was gained by the creation of curriculum associates or curriculum coordinators in the two districts.

Did the districts effect any economies by their experiments? In an era of "taxpayer revolts," administrators must examine their budgets carefully, searching for categories in which expenditures might be reduced. One possible category covers the allocation of funds for supporting department heads with released time and salary increments. It is clear, however, that no savings were achieved in either the Berkeley or Whittier experiments. The associates and coordinators in those districts were just as expensive to support as were the traditional department heads whom they replaced. No savings were to be achieved by concentrating expenditures for released time or salary increments into a few positions. It is true that a net reduction in costs resulted from the fact that only one curriculum coordinator was established in each school in the Whittier district at the time of the author's visit there, but that was clearly a temporary situation. The superintendent and his staff were emphatic in their determination to increase the number of coordinators as soon as the district's financial situation permitted.

Did the associates or coordinators render services which eliminated the need for the traditional department head position? Again, the answer seems unmistakably negative. Department chairmen were still needed in both districts to coordinate, guide, and assist teachers in their individual subject areas. This need was most clearly demonstrated when the department head position, supported by released time and a salary increment, had to be re-established at Berkeley High School to meet the needs of the faculty there.

Did the associates or coordinators render services which were beyond the ability of department heads in most districts to perform, considering the limitations imposed on their operations by the generally inadequate training and support made available to them? Here, in the author's opinion, the answer is clearly affirmative.

The author believes, however, that good department heads can render similarly broader services if the conditions under which they generally operate are improved. The author is convinced that if administrators will accept the recommendations made in this book, they will enable their department heads to function with maximum effectiveness. And when such superior levels of performance are achieved, districts will find that the regular department head will continue to meet the needs of his teachers and his subject discipline in the future, just as he has tried to do in the past.

EVALUATING THE DIVISION PLAN

A final and frequently reported variation on the traditional practice of maintaining subject area departments with individual chairmen is the division plan. This plan organizes schools into units of related subject areas by merging individual departments into larger groupings such as "humanities" or "fine arts." In such schools, the customary ten to twelve department heads are replaced by perhaps five division heads, each supervising a unit which combines two, three, or even more separate subject fields.

Why is the division plan being studied and, in some cases, tested in school districts throughout the country? Proponents of this organizational system claim the following as some of the advantages which it offers over the traditional departmental plan: [17]

1. Divisions being founded on broader principles than are single-subject departments, tend to promote better correlation of instruction. (The theory is that when teachers of related subjects such as American history and American literature are brought together in the same organizational unit, they will be more apt to devise ways of relating their courses more closely to each other.)

2. Divisions lessen duplication of effort among departments, creating a more unified program at lower cost. (Continuing the above illustration, the two instructors might streamline their respective courses by eliminating material from one that has already been presented in the other. The English teacher, for example, no longer has to discuss the historical backgrounds of the literature which he teaches, since he is sure that this material has already been presented in U.S. History classes.)

3. Divisions pool the talents and energies of teachers into larger units, where they may be more efficiently supervised. (In many schools, there may be too few teachers in certain subject areas—notably music, art, homemaking, and other such electives—to justify establishing department head positions with released time for them. As a result, these departments may suffer continually from lack of unifying direction. When such small units are grouped into divisions, however, it becomes easier to justify the cost of providing them with the kind of leadership which they require and deserve. Furthermore, a division head who speaks for a dozen or more teachers may well find his recommendations concerning curriculum, finances, or general policy carry more weight in school and district committees than they did when he represented only three or four teachers.)

4. Principals may become more involved in directing
    the instructional program of a school organized by
    divisions than a school organized by departments.
    (Administrators may find it easier to work with a
    few division heads than with a larger number of
    department heads, each of whom may reflect only
    a single curricular viewpoint.)

Divisions have been established in a number of schools in the
United states, particularly in the Chicago area and on the Pacific
Coast. In an example of one such changeover to the division
plan, the principal of Rich Township High School in Park Forest,
Illinois, replaced eleven department chairmen with four division
heads. The divisions created in that school were for humanities,
mathematics-science, physical education, and the related arts.

Does the division plan represent the organizational system of
the schools of the future? Will the department head of today
evolve into the division head of tomorrow?

While conducting his study of the department head position,
the author discussed the potential of the division plan with
administrators and teachers in a score of districts in California and
Oregon. A few schools in these districts had established experimental divisions. Other systems were still examining the question
in meetings of district study committees. Still others had rejected
the division concept. As might be expected, the author received
many different opinions concerning the potential strengths and
weaknesses inherent in the division plan.

One administrator in a small, wealthy suburban district near
San Francisco saw many benefits to be derived from combining
departments into divisions. He affirmed the point made earlier in
this section that a district might find it easier to provide released
time for a division head than for the head of a small department.
He also pointed out that divisions might provide for better
curriculum planning and "cross-fertilization" of teacher talents,
thus reducing the possibility that teachers would feel isolated
within individual subject areas. He also saw the possibility that
divisions could encourage greater use of school libraries as resource
centers for individualized, inter-disciplinary study, since the contents of such libraries cut across departmental lines. And he

suggested that this organizational pattern might help to individu-
alize learning because students who are stronger in one of the
subjects represented in a division could more easily apply this
strength to help them in other areas in the division, where their
talents might not be so great.

A principal in southern California saw the division plan working
particularly well in the fields of art, music, and drama. He asserted
that teachers in those subjects tend to be such individualists, with
such highly specialized skills, that their individual programs would
not suffer if they were merged under a single coordinator. On a
more positive note, he pointed out that having a division head to
guide the work of these smaller departments improves communication among them, which is particularly valuable when they need
to combine their talents to produce a play or other fine arts
program. In this principal's own school, a fine arts division had
been established, combining the fields of art, music, and drama.
The person selected to serve as division head in this school was the
teacher from one of those three areas who had the highest degree
of organizational skill.

Not all of the administrators and teachers interviewed by the
author were in favor of the division plan, however. An assistant
superintendent in a district on the San Francisco peninsula which
is famed for the high quality of its staff and its programs took a
more cautious approach to the possible advantages to be gained by
merging departments into divisions. He felt that inter-disciplinary
teams might occur naturally in special teaching programs designed
for particular types of students (especially the remedial student),
but he believed that the individual teachers in those teams should
remain in their separate subject area departments. He asserted that
only rarely can an individual be found to serve as division head
who has sufficient competency to work in more than one field.
Without such competency, a division head will not be accepted as
a real curricular and instructional leader by teachers in the division
who work outside of his area of particular specialization.

Interestingly enough, one school in that administrator's district
was experimenting with the division plan when the author visited
it, and the "curriculum associates" in charge of two particular
divisions illustrated the superintendent's point perfectly.

One of these men, in charge of the fine arts division, had an exceptional background of training and experience in both music and art. As a result, the teachers in those areas with whom the author spoke seemed to accept this individual's leadership enthusiastically. They also appreciated the fact that they now belonged to a larger organizational unit, whose spokesman thus carried greater weight when he discussed questions of school programs, policies, and, of course, budgets.

On the other hand, the head of the avocational arts division, which included industrial arts, homemaking, and business education, admitted quite candidly that he could offer little leadership to the teachers outside of his own field, which happened to be industrial arts. The same was true of even the best teachers in the other subject areas combined within this division: the homemaking teacher in no way felt qualified to speak on matters concerning the school's metal shop classes, nor was even the most experienced industrial arts teacher prepared to offer curricular leadership in the fields of foods and clothing. As a result, this "division" existed in name only and functioned as a coordinated unit only on an administrative chart. In fact, the position of "division head" was regularly rotated among the lead teachers in each of the three subject areas combined within it. As each of these people held the position in turn, he merely rubber-stamped the policies and requisitions originating from the teachers outside his own specialty field, preferring to devote all of his time to working in the area where he felt competent to provide leadership.

In the author's opinion, this school's experience points up the major arguments against the division plan:[18]

1. Division heads face the near-impossible task of trying to keep abreast of curricular and instructional developments in a variety of subject fields. (Department heads know how difficult this is to do within just a single subject.)

2. Division heads must possess the relatively rare gift of being able to supervise teachers in quite diverse classroom situations and subject areas if they are to provide the kind of leadership which constitutes a primary responsibility of the effective school department head.

3. Division heads must necessarily work with larger groups of teachers than department heads do. (Consequently, they may be less well-known to their colleagues and less accessible to individual teachers who need help—especially help of a highly specific nature—in their work.)

In view of these facts, does the division plan really offer a desirable alternative to the traditional departmental system of school organization? Administrators who are considering the possibility that their own school departments may evolve into divisions in the future must weigh that question carefully.

The answer may lie in the results of a research study conducted by school administrators in the high school district at Arlington Heights, Illinois. [19] They decided to evaluate the relative merits of the division and the department by studying the two organizational plans in operation in high schools located near Chicago.

In order to make an effective comparison between the two organizational systems, the administrators had first to devise a suitable evaluation instrument. They began this task by developing a list of fifteen principles which they believed should apply in any effective plan for school organization. They stated these principles as follows:

1. The secondary school organization permits each person to have only one superior to whom he is directly responsible. Each staff member should, therefore, report to and be supervised by a single administrative officer.

2. The secondary school organization allows the channels of communication to be definitely known to all concerned. The structure of the organization should facilitate communication and promote cooperative understanding.

3. The secondary school organization should be such that it utilizes maximally the time and energy of each member.

4. The secondary school organization should facilitate maximum cooperation among the members of the organization. It should allow all members of the

staff to function as coordinated parts rather than as individuals.

5. The secondary school organization provides that each unit and each administrative officer be held directly accountable for the proper discharge of his responsibilities. The functions, responsibilities, and working relationships of each staff member should be clearly defined and understood and should be recognized in actual practice. The area of responsibility assigned to each person should be reasonable in scope.

6. The secondary organization allows the duties and responsibilities assigned to one person to be homogeneous. Such responsibilities and duties utilize fully the talents and abilities of each member.

7. The secondary school organization permits authority to act to be delegated to individuals who have been given responsibility. Authority should be commensurate with the assignment of responsibility. Responsibilities and authority should be distributed among individuals in a manner consistent with the purposes of the school.

8. The secondary school organization facilitates democratic procedure. Operation should be based on the appropriate participation of the entire educational staff, the parents, and the students.

9. The secondary school organization provides for all essential programs, services, and activities. The organization must facilitate the attainment of the desired educational goals.

10. The secondary school organization recognizes the principal as the key person in the educational enterprise. It recognizes him as an instructional leader, staff officer, and head of his faculty.

11. The secondary school organization recognizes the teacher as the basic operative of the school system. While others deal with instruction, the teacher is primarily concerned with that function.

12. The secondary school organization makes possible the utilization of supervisors, coordinators, or specialists as helpers and counselors of teachers on special problems. In no case should they be charged with line or authoritative functions such as evaluating the competency of teachers or the direction of school programs.

13. The secondary school organization allows adminstrative personnel to lead, stimulate, coordinate, serve, and appraise instead of inspect and command. Line officers should be generalists with broad areas of responsibilities.

14. The secondary school organization provides for continuous and cooperative evaluation and redirection of the organization.

15. The secondary school organization provides for inservice training and for the professional growth of all members.

This list of fifteen principles was then given to a group of teachers in the Arlington high school system who were asked to develop lists of specific actions or behaviors which would tend to carry the principles into effect. Questionnaires were then devised to measure the extent to which the actions described by the teachers did take place in schools which were operated by departments and schools which were organized into divisions. These questionnaires were distributed to teachers in eight Chicago area high schools, four of which were organized along departmental lines and four by divisions.

The results obtained from this survey showed that of the fifteen principles established above, seven operated equally well in division schools and department schools. Of the remaining eight principles, however, only one was found to operate more effectively through the division structure. The other seven were found functioning to a greater degree in schools organized into individual subject area departments.

Specifically, the eight principles which reflected a critical difference between the two organizational systems produced the following comparison of the strengths and weaknesses of departments, as measured against divisions:

1. Departmental organization, to a greater degree

than divisional organization, permits each teacher to have only one superior to whom he is responsible.

2. Departmental organization better facilitates communication among teachers.

3. Departmental organization allows members of the staff to function as more coordinated parts of a whole than does organization by divisions.

4. Departmental organization allows for greater accountability for the discharge of duties.

5. Departmental organization more fully utilizes the talents of individual teachers in particular subject matter areas.

6. Departmental organization better provides for all essential programs, services, and activities in the school.

7. Departmental organization utilizes supervisors, coordinators, and specialists more effectively as helpers of teachers.

8. Organization by divisions shows its superiority over organization by departments *only* in providing more effectively for continuous and cooperative evaluation and possible redirection of the school's total program.

Several other conclusions were drawn from this thorough and detailed comparison of the two organizational systems. One was that the division plan might not have been in operation in the particular schools selected for the study long enough to have proved itself. Another was that it would probably be better to develop a division-structured school from the beginning, with the opening of a new facility in a district, than to change an established, departmentalized school into a school organized by divisions.

But perhaps the clearest answer to the question of whether the division head will be the effective school department head of the future lies in this conclusion reported in the Arlington study just cited:

"School districts presently organized on the departmental plan should be careful about suddenly deciding to adopt the division structure. Districts that have done so apparently have not solved the problems attributed to departmental organization. It does not appear that communication, coordination, and supervision are improved. The division concept seems to facilitate evaluation and redirection, but at the same time appears to weaken the effective operation of the other principles. [20]

AFFIRMING THE REALITY OF
THE DEPARTMENT HEAD'S FUTURE

The examples discussed in this chapter indicate that a number of school districts are studying the possible merits of expanding the traditional role and function of the subject area department head. Is there evidence of a trend away from the departmental system of organization and toward any of the innovative plans cited here?

From what the author has been able to determine, through visitations and research, the answer is, emphatically, "No!"

A final piece of evidence to support this conclusion is a survey of attitudes and expectations toward department heads, covering public high schools in the North Central Association of Colleges and Secondary Schools.[21] Responses to this survey were received from the principals of 273 schools, covering nearly a score of states, which employed 40 or more teachers. The study obtained the following conclusive results:

1. There was widespread use of department heads in the schools which responded. Approximately 80 percent of these schools indicated that they employed department heads; and this figure reached 98 per cent in schools which employed 100 or more teachers! More than two-thirds of even the smallest schools, those with 40 to 69 instructors on their staffs, reported that they maintained department head positions.

2. There was *no* trend away from the use of department heads nor toward combining several subject

areas into divisions. In fact, schools seemed to be establishing even more specialized departments, rather than grouping existing ones.

3. There was *no* widespread dissatisfaction with the departmental system of organization. Ninety-seven per cent of the principals in schools which had department heads indicated that they would re-establish departments if they were reorganizing schools similar to their present ones. Furthermore, approximately 90 per cent of the teachers and principals surveyed rejected the proposition that schools would be better off without department heads. In general, teachers, department heads, and principals alike indicated that chairmen would provide effective supervision if they were given the necessary time and authority for doing the job.

The authors of this study drew the following significant conclusion from the results of their survey:

"In summary, these studies seem to explode some myths about the department head position as it exists in the larger public high schools. Some of these *unfounded myths* are: (1) that there is a trend away from the use of department heads in the larger secondary schools; (2) that the division organization is replacing the departmental organization; and (3) that there is widespread dissatisfaction with the position among department heads, teachers, or principals. It can be concluded from these studies that the departmental organization is typical rather than atypical in the larger high schools, and that teachers and principals alike view departmental organization as offering considerable potential for effective supervision and administration."[22]

A TIMETABLE FOR IMPROVING
THE DEPARTMENT HEAD POSITION

Thus it appears that the subject area department head will continue to play a key role in the school of tomorrow, just as he does in the school of today. Administrators who are seeking to improve their schools in order to prepare for that tomorrow should, therefore, focus a substantial part of their efforts on seeking to improve the position of their department chairmen.

The recommendations outlined in the preceding chapters form the cornerstone for a program designed to accomplish such improved effectiveness. These suggested policies and practices mark the major steps in a cycle which begins with improved selection procedures and continues through to improved evaluation policies for school department heads.

Administrators who wish to adopt these recommendations might follow the timetable outlined below for phasing in their implementation:

Time Period	Actions to Be Accomplished
Fall Semester, First Year	Administrators and department heads in a district review the policies and practices recommended in this book. They decide to adopt these recommendations and move toward their implementation.
Spring Semester, First Year	1. THE PROCEDURES RECOMMENDED FOR SELECTING NEW DEPARTMENT HEADS GO INTO EFFECT *(Chapter 6)*. 2. The teaching schedules for department heads in each school during the coming semester are arranged so that released periods coincide *(Chapter 8)*. 3. Administrators review their allocation of non-certificated staff time in each school, so as to increase support for department heads where possible *(Chapter 7)*. 4. Department heads are notified that they must have completed at least one course or approved workshop program dealing with the principles and practices of effective supervision of instruction within three years of this date *(Chapter 6)*.
Fall Semester, Second Year	1. DEPARTMENT HEAD RELEASED AND PREPARATION PERIODS ARE SCHEDULED CONCURRENTLY FROM THIS TIME ON. 2. ADDITIONAL CLERICAL AND CUSTODIAL ASSISTANCE IS ASSIGNED TO DEPARTMENT HEADS WHERE DESIRABLE AND POSSIBLE FROM THIS TIME ON.

3. Administrators and department heads establish guide-
    lines for in-service training programs, to go into effect
    in each school as soon as possible *(Chapter 6)*.

4. Administrators and department heads establish objec-
    tives and programs of activities for district councils, to
    begin meeting regularly during the coming spring
    semester *(Chapter 8)*.

Spring Semester, 1. DISTRICT COUNCILS OF DEPARTMENT HEADS
                          ORGANIZE AND MEET REGULARLY FROM THIS
Second Year   TIME ON.

2. IN-SERVICE TRAINING PROGRAMS FOR
    DEPARTMENT HEADS BEGIN TO OPERATE IN
    EACH SCHOOL AND CONTINUE FROM THIS
    TIME ON.

Fall Semester, 1. One district council is selected to produce a pilot
                       training and operations manual for department heads
Third Year   in that subject area during a workshop to be held
                       during the coming summer *(Chapter 6)*.

2. Administrators and department heads establish guide-
    lines and programs of activities for department heads
    in one district school who will receive extended duty
    contracts in the fall of the fourth year *(Chapter 8)*.

3. Policies and practices governing the annual evaluation
    of department head performance in each school are
    discussed by administrators and department heads.
    The initial evaluation will be conducted during the
    coming spring semester *(Chapter 10)*.

Spring Semester, 1. The first trial run of multi-level department head
                         evaluation is conducted.
Third Year

Summer, 1. The first district council prepares a manual for depart-
                 ment heads in that subject area.
Third Year

Fall Semester, 1. Administrators and department heads begin to review
                       policies governing released time and salary increments
Fourth Year   for department heads *(Chapter 7)*.

2. The first department head manual is evaluated.
3. The results of the first performance evaluations are studied.
4. Extended duty contracts are issued to department heads in one school.

Spring Semester, 1. REGULAR ANNUAL MULTI-LEVEL EVALUATIONS OF DEPARTMENT HEAD PER-
Fourth Year FORMANCE ARE CONDUCTED FROM THIS TIME ON; PROGRAMS ARE ESTABLISHED TO COR-RECT EVIDENCES OF DEFECTIVE PERFOR-MANCE.
2. The requirement for periodic department head training in concepts and techniques of supervision is evaluated; the requirement is either deleted or ESTAB-LISHED AS A REGULAR, FIVE-YEAR REQUIRE-MENT FOR CONTINUED APPOINTMENT TO DEPARTMENT HEAD POSITIONS

Summer, 1. Department heads with extended contracts are on duty in a designated district school.
Fourth Year

Fall Semester, 1. IMPROVEMENTS CONSISTENT WITH AVAILA-BLE RESOURCES ARE EFFECTED IN DISTRICT
Fifth Year POLICIES RELATING TO RELEASED TIME AND SALARY INCREMENTS FOR DEPARTMENT HEADS; THESE IMPROVEMENTS ARE TO BE REVIEWED FROM THIS TIME ON.
2. A second district council is selected to produce a de-partment head manual during the coming summer.
3. Activities of department heads who served on ex-tended duty contracts during the preceding year are evaluated; department heads in another school are se-lected to receive such contracts in the fall of the sixth year.

Spring Semester, 1. Administrators and department heads begin to develop guidelines for a limited number of coordinating
Fifth Year department head, resident curriculum associate, or

teacher executive positions, to be established during
the seventh year *(Chapter 9)*.

— —

Sixth Year   1. Guidelines for the special positions described above
are reviewed, applications are solicited, and appoint-
ments are made, effective the following fall semester.
2. The second department head manual is evaluated.
3. The activities of the second group of department
heads on extended duty contracts are evaluated.
EXTENDED DUTY CONTRACTS WILL BE ISSUED
REGULARLY TO DEPARTMENT HEADS IN THE
FUTURE, AS DISTRICT RESOURCES PERMIT.

— —

Seventh Year   1. Department heads in special leadership positions begin
their periods of service.
2. Administrators, department heads, and general faculty
begin to review and evaluate the effectiveness of the
recommendations adopted during the preceding years
to improve department head performance. Necessary
changes are made as district experiences require, and
additional new policies (suggested by the district staff)
are adopted. A CONTINUOUS AND ON-GOING
PROGRAM IS THUS ESTABLISHED FOR THE
IMPROVEMENT OF *ALL* DISTRICT INSTRUC-
TIONAL PROGRAMS.

APPENDIX

APPENDIX "A"

A Model In-Service Training Program for Department Heads

REPORT OF THE CURRICULUM ASSOCIATES WORKSHOP*

Redwood High School

Tamalpais Union High School District

Larkspur, California

*Reprinted by permission of the Tamalpais Union High School District

205

CURRICULUM ASSOCIATES WORKSHOP

RESOURCES

During the workshop there were several special resources made available which greatly increased the value of the workshop. These resources fell into three major categories: resource speakers, field trips, and professional library material.

RESOURCE SPEAKERS

Dr. Robert E. McLean, Principal of Henry Gunn High School, Palo Alto Unified School District, Palo Alto, California.

Dr. McLean opened Gunn High School the Fall of 1964 at which time he instituted the Curriculum Associates concept of school organization. He also introduced many other kinds of innovations, most of which were concerned with student management and control. Curricular innovations were also introduced of a non-graded nature. Dr. McLean spent one day with the workshop discussing his ideas and how they have worked for the past three years in his school.

Mr. Robert Shutes, Assistant Principal, Palo Alto Senior High School, Palo Alto Unified School District, Palo Alto, California.

Mr. Shutes has served as Assistant Principal at Palo Alto for the past several years, during which time he instituted the Curriculum Associates concept and conducted a modified workshop for Curriculum Associates. In the organization of the school he is responsible for the work of instruction. Mr. Shutes discussed with us the research available in the field of learning theory. He assisted materially in preparing our workshop bibliography, and he presented many of his own research papers on learning theory to our workshop.

Dr. James Cooper, Supervisor of Stanford Intern Program, Stanford University, Stanford, California.

Dr. Cooper is currently supervisor of the *micro-teaching phase* of the Stanford Intern Teaching Program. He discussed this program with us and presented material on the micro-teaching technique as it might be applied for in-service teacher training. He was responsible for the arrangements for a field trip to Stanford University to see the micro-teaching technique in operation. Dr. Cooper also addressed himself to the larger uses of television in instruction. He discussed the concept of the differentiated staff as well, particularly as it relates to the Curriculum Associates concept of school organization.

FIELD TRIPS

The members of the workshop participated in two field trips during the course of the workshop. The first of these was to the Micro-Teaching Center for Stanford University. This was located in the Escondido School of the Palo Alto Unified School District on the Stanford University campus. At this school, the television equipment was installed for the micro-teaching sessions planned for the fall group of Stanford Intern teachers. Members of the workshop had the opportunity to participate in the use of this equipment.

The second field trip was taken to the Interviewer Training Center of Pacific Telephone Company in downtown San Francisco. Under the direction of Mr. K. E. Hettick and his staff, members of the workshop participated in an interview training session as conducted by Pacific Telephone.

PROFESSIONAL LIBRARY MATERIAL

The Professional Library of the Tamalpais Union High School District furnished a complete selection of books and periodicals as requested by our workshop. The full bibliography is contained in the section of this report under Workshop Bibliography and Materials.

SCHEDULE

The following is a day-by-day breakdown of the activities of the workshop. In this breakdown the topics discussed have been indicated, and the participants other than those of the workshop identified.

Monday   Faculty Lounge   1:00 p.m. to 5:00 p.m.

1. General review of the workshop schedule, assignment of reading from the bibliography, assignment of reports to be made, and general purpose of the workshop stated.

2. Resource speaker, Dr. Robert McLean, Principal, Gunn High School.
   Profile of Gunn High School; rationale for Curriculum Associates organization; unique aspects of student management, class bells, attendance recording, and hall passes; curriculum innovations; special resources available to teachers.

Tuesday   Faculty Lounge   1:00 p.m. to 5:00 p.m.

1. Review of reading assignments made from workshop

bibliography, reference to report guide in workshop materials.

2. Resource speaker, Mr. Robert Shutes, Assistant Principal, Palo Alto Senior High School.
Profile of Palo Alto Senior High School; role of Curriculum Associate at Palo Alto High School; importance of learning theory and research on learning theory; discussion of sample research bulletins.

Wednesday   Faculty Lounge   1:00 p.m. to 5:00 p.m.
1. Presentation of film, *No Reason to Stay*. Story of bright student who drops out of school because of dissatisfaction with instruction.

2. Resource speaker, Dr. James Cooper, Stanford University.
Presentation of micro-teaching, a new framework for in-service education; description of Stanford program for developing specific teaching skill through micro-teaching; general use of television recordings as a new dimension in teacher education; discussion of the differentiated teaching staff and the role of the Curriculum Associate in this framework; preparation for field trip visit to Stanford University to observe Micro-Teaching Center.

Thursday   Escondido School   10:00 a.m. to 3:30 p.m.
1. Field trip to Escondido School on the Stanford University campus.
Observed tapes of micro-teaching technique; discussed facilities and equipment involved; had Curriculum Associates Raymond Kemper, Charles Kurtz, and Louise Velte present sample teaching for video-tape; reviewed and critiqued above three lessons; discussed in-service education possibilities of micro-teaching.
Dr. James Cooper conducted the Micro-Teaching Laboratory during the field trip. Redwood Mathematics Instructor and Audio-Visual equipment Supervisor Fred Broemmer accompanied the workshop members on the field trip to observe the technical aspects of the equipment used in the micro-teaching technique.

Friday   Faculty Lounge   1:00 p.m. to 5:00 p.m.

1. General review of ideas and concepts presented by speakers
    and programs during the past week; general open discussion
    on specific recommendations for changes at Redwood;
    prolonged and open criticism of present system and sugges-
    tions for change.

Monday   Faculty Lounge   1:00 p.m. to 5:00 p.m.

1. Reports by individual members of the reading assignments
    given from the workshop bibliography; discussion of
    reports, suggestions for changes at Redwood that have
    emerged from the reports.

2. Discussion of present new teacher requirement procedures;
    discussion of how to select the best teachers, what we look
    for, what information is needed; preparation for field trip
    to Pacific Telephone Company Interviewer Training Center;
    discussion of interview techniques needed for good teacher
    selection.

Tuesday   Pacific Telephone Company 1:00 p.m. to 5:00 p.m.

1. Lunch at Pacific Telephone Company; introduction to
    Interviewer Training staff as headed by Mr. K. E. Hettick,
    General Employment Manager.

2. Visit to Interviewer Training Center of Pacific Telephone;
    discussion of "How to Select a Good Teacher;" develop-
    mental session; mock interview, Curriculum Associate
    Ronald Hurt conducting the interview; critique of the
    interview, discussion and conclusions; emphasis of deter-
    mining what it is you are looking for before you interview
    for it.

Wednesday   Faculty Lounge   1:00 p.m. to 5:00 p.m.

1. Review of Administrative Organizational Pattern for
    Redwood; discussion of changes; agreement on modified
    organizational plan.

2. Reports from Administrators on their relationship to Cur-
    riculum Associates; Assistant Principal on management,
    budget, control; Dean of Adult and Summer Schools on
    tie-in of these programs with regular Day School; Dean of
    Pupil Personnel report on Data Processing services, Coun-
    seling services, grouping and tracking of students.

Thursday   Faculty Lounge   1:00 p.m. to 5:00 p.m.

1. Continuation of Administrator's reports; Dean of Boys and
    Dean of Girls on tardies, attendance, single period absences,
    discipline; discussion of more positive contacts for Deans;
    recommendations for further study and implication of
    counseling to this study.

2. Reports from individual departments on new programs in
    the following areas: curriculum changes and innovations,
    staff growth and development, in-service education pro-
    grams for teachers, supervision plans and schedules, budg-
    etary needs and goals, facility plans and needs, and
    instructional material needs. General discussion of the
    relationship of given departments to all other departments
    in the above-mentioned areas.

Friday   Faculty Lounge   1:00 p.m. to 5:00 p.m.

1. Continuation of individual department reports; prolonged
    discussion of use of pass-fail grades for certain departments,
    (i.e. Boys and Girls P.E.); continued discussion of school-
    wide implications in departmental reports.

2. Summation of workshop and discussion of format for the
    report of the workshop; discussion of general recommen-
    dations affecting all departments, consensus on these
    recommendations.

RECOMMENDATIONS FOR INSTRUCTION

The recommendations of the workshop have been presented in the
following format: first, the basic goal to be achieved has been stated, and
then, specific procedures designed to achieve that goal have been articulated.

1. There needs to be a greater awareness on the part of the
    instructional staff of the increased number of new teaching
    methodologies and techniques in the fields of learning
    theory and teaching.

    A. Curriculum Associates will initiate a series of intra-
        department classroom visitations with an aim toward
        sharing ideas on teaching and to learn from the
        strengths of each other.

    B. Curriculum Associates will initiate inter-departmental
        meetings with other departments within the school to
        work toward the solution of common curricular and
        instructional problems.

C. The Faculty Library will be strengthened and augmented with materials on learning theory and research on teaching, and periodic research bulletins will be distributed to staff members when appropriate.

D. Curriculum Associates will initiate in-service education programs within their departments aimed at the strengthening of teaching. The use of the video tape recorder and micro-teaching is seen as one effective kind of in-service program.

2. There needs to be an increased sensitivity on the part of the instructional staff to the total needs of students and student behavior.

A. The Principal shall initiate an in-service program for the faculty with an emphasis on the nature and behavior of students today.

B. The Deans of Boys and Girls shall initiate more positive contact with teachers through departments aimed at establishing a closer liaison with the teaching staff as a whole. The aim of their program shall be to serve as resource to in-service programs designed to establish a good learning climate in the classroom.

3. There needs to be continued emphasis on the development of a quality teaching staff for the school.

A. With the aid of all members of the staff, a description of what is the good teacher will be developed. This criterion will serve as a guideline to the recruitment and selection of new teachers and the appraisal and evaluation of present staff members.

B. The recruitment and selection procedures for new staff members will continue to involve the Curriculum Associates. Increased data will be obtained on each candidate, that data to include, if possible, a transcript of college record.

C. The Curriculum Associate will assume an even greater role in the assignment of teachers and the development of the schedule of classes for a given department.

4. There needs to be a stronger relationship between the educational objectives of the Summer School Curriculum and the Regular Day School Curriculum.

A.   The Dean of Adult and Summer Schools will initiate
a Summer School Steering Committee composed of
the Curriculum Associates, a teacher from each
department, and himself, to develop a substantial
summer program and an evaluation of the existing
program.

ENGLISH DEPARTMENT

CURRICULUM CHANGES

The Language and Composition Workshop of the Summer of 19 __ will
bring into focus three years of district-wide research in linguistics and
rhetoric. This will mean extensive and immediate changes in existing course
content and methods.

Two sections of the new elective, "The Art of Film," will begin in
September, 19__.

Redwood English teachers will continue their study of the possibility of
an entirely elective English program. The Committee on Electives has met
several times and will continue to explore this idea during 19 __.

The department plans to continue discussion and research on ability
grouping within the English program. For 19 _-_, the following modifi-
cations will be made: The "Y" English program at the English 5-6 level will
be eliminated; the number of "X" students has been reduced; and two
experimental English 7-8 classes with heterogeneous grouping have been
established to test the values of heterogeneous grouping.

The department is interested in the possibilities of longer blocks of time
periodically for particular language activities, and the establishing of some
type of flexible schedule which would not require the need to see students
daily.

Experiments with WEEP student aides in the classroom during 19_-_
were successful. It is planned to expand this program as able students are
identified who are especially interested in English and teaching.

STAFF DEVELOPMENT

During 19_-_, four grade-level chairmen were appointed to help with
book rotation, film scheduling, and grade-level curriculum. It is intended to
expand this delegative process. In addition, during 19_-_ four teachers will
be assigned one period each in the Library as resource teachers. By this, it is
hoped to encourage innovations in small group instruction, independent
study, and expanded use of library facilities.

IN-SERVICE PROGRAM

The department is accumulating a large professional library with the help of NDEA funds. This will add significantly this year to the reference collection.

SUPERVISION

In a recent department meeting, a plan was initiated for frequent, informal visits to each other's classes. In this plan, every teacher visits whenever he wants to, after making advance arrangements with another teacher.

BUDGET AND FACILITY NEEDS

There exists a shortage of several capital outlay items: film projectors, overhead projectors, record players, and tape records. This shortage tends to retard meaningful and purposeful developments in method and curriculum.

The department tested use of the overhead projector in the teaching of language and found it a valuable asset to inductive instruction in composition.

The department is working with ways to meet the shortage of office and classroom space. During 19__-__, the four resource teachers, who will also be traveling teachers, will have desks in the Library. It is felt that the most effective way to meet the next few years' immediate overcrowding would be to provide each English classroom with an overhead projector and to increase the number of film projectors and other A-V equipment so that it will be easier for the traveling teachers.

SCIENCE DEPARTMENT

CURRICULUM CHANGES

There is a need to develop a twelfth grade science course for those students who began the science sequence as freshmen. It is possible that this course will be of the advanced placement type with an emphasis in Biology or Chemistry.

The Foundations of Science course will be reviewed in the light of several new curricula now available for slow learners.

IN-SERVICE PROGRAMS

During 19__-__, all members of the department will be requested to attend at least one major science conference and report back to the other

members of the department with regard to any interesting ideas or developments they derived from the conferences.

Plans have been made to meet as a department at least once a semester
with the deans and with the counseling staff.

The Curriculum Associate will ask all members of the department to make
a serious effort to visit both his class and as many of his fellow teachers as
proves feasible during the year and the Curriculum Associate will undertake
regualr visitations of all members of the department.

BUDGETARY NEEDS

The most important budgetary need for the immediate future pertains to
the necessity of remodeling and equipping the new science room to be
located in the present Mechanical Drawing room. Adequate capital outlay
funds will need to be allocated to properly equip this new facility in 19__-__ .

There is a continuing need for audio-visual equipment such as overhead
projectors, sets of prepared transparencies, and motion picture projection
equipment.

GIRLS PHYSICAL EDUCATION DEPARTMENT

CURRICULUM CHANGES

The department plans to continue and expand its program of student
teaching for junior and senior girls within the department.

The Narcotics unit will be retained and developed to include other major
health and social problems. This program will be expanded beyond the
freshman level.

Consideration will be given to a pass-fail type of grading.

With the advent of tennis courts, this activity will be integrated into the
instructional program.

IN-SERVICE PROGRAMS

All department members will be encouraged to participate in the newly
formed Marin County Chapter of CAHPER (California Association of Health,
Physical Education and Recreation). The department will continue its
program of sharing information regarding subject matter in health and
physical education.

In terms of supervision, the department will concentrate on observing and
assisting teachers throughout the year on a give and take basis.

BUDGETARY NEEDS

Additional gymnastics apparatus, track and field equipment, aquatic equipment, are examples of needs that will enhance the program. Additional bulletin boards, including at least one glass enclosed board, are also needed. Audio-visual equipment needs to be added to the department, particularly a 16 mm projector.

BOYS PHYSICAL EDUCATION DEPARTMENT

CURRICULUM CHANGES

All freshmen students will take part in the core program which includes all activities in addition to first aid, fitness testing and vision testing. Sophomores, juniors and seniors will be on an elective program. During a three-year period, they must take swimming, weight training, two individual activities, and two recreation activities. Each activity will last six weeks. One semester will have three six-week blocks. Consideration will be given to grading all courses on a pass-fail basis.

The shortened period will require a change in the dressing and showering time for boys. Boys this year will have only a five-minute dressing period.

IN-SERVICE PROGRAMS

All members of the department will be encouraged to attend at least one physical education conference, as well as to enroll in one new course in the field.

A program of inter-school visitation augmented by inter-class visitation will be initiated by the Curriculum Associate. In addition to observation of each other's classes, assignments within the department will be rotated each six weeks.

BUDGETARY NEEDS

Additional funds will be needed to bring the weight training program up to the level desired by the department.

The department will request consideration of the building of a portable classroom behind the gym to use for first aid, narcotics instruction, and general classroom use.

As the athletic program expands to include girls athletics as well, the need for a field house becomes more and more apparent.

LIBRARY

NEW COLLECTIONS

In the area of printed resources, the Library intends to expand the collection of course-oriented, multiple-copy books, mostly paperbacks.

The tape collection will be expanded and the Library will initiate a records collection.

New collections in microfilms (magazines, historical documents) will be the next priority. While inexpensive in itself, microfilm requires reader-projectors which will require a heavy capital outlay for four to seven readers needed for active use.

Finally, the Library hopes to begin a collection of prints (art repro-ductions), film loops, and video-tapes as part of an integrated collection of learning resources.

NEW SERVICES

A materials production area and staff, organized for the 19 _-_ school year, will provide certain kinds of services to teachers eight hours a day through the central access the Library can provide.

A new photocopy service to students and faculty with improved quality and reduced costs will be available.

Additional library space for faculty library, office and work areas will be developed this fall as the Library works cooperatively and experimentally with departments. An enlarged listening area will be developed mid-year, 19_-_.

The TV and Radio Guide will be continued and expanded. This service is patterned after college library services under the name SDI (Selective Dissemination of Information).

BUDGETARY NEEDS

Micro-film readers, audio-visual equipment and other kinds of equipment will be needed to implement the programs and services outlined above.

Subject matter resource areas will be created within the Library by rearrangement of the book collection. Two areas will be defined as follows: English, Social Studies, and Foreign Language as one area, and Mathematics and Science as the other area. Some accoustical treatment will be required to make the use of these areas effective.

WORKSHOP BIBLIOGRAPHY AND MATERIALS

The following workshop bibliography was used as a basis for the workshop research bulletins that have been reported as part of this report.

Bellack, Arno A., editor, *Theory and Research in Teaching*, "Toward a Theory of Teaching," B. Othanel Smith, pp 1-10.

Bulletin of the National Association of Secondary School Principals, "Effective Teaching and Personal Potential," December 1966, pp 10-114.

Bulletin of the National Association of Secondary School Principals, "Radio and Television in the Secondary School," October 1966, pp 65-220.

Bulletin of the National Association of Secondary School Principals, "Some Challenges of Curricular Change," September 1966, pp 9-21.

Gage, N. L., *Handbook of Research on Teaching.* Rand McNally & Co., 1963, Chapter 10: "Analysis and Investigation of Teaching Methods," pp 448-505.

Hilgard, Ernest R., *Theories of Learning and Instruction.* University of Chicago Press, 1964, Chapter 8, "The Teacher's Role in the Motivation of the Learner," pp 182-209.

Krathwohl, David R., and others, *Taxonomy of Educational Objectives,* David McKay Co., Inc., 1956, Appendix A & B, pp 176-193.

Perceiving, Behaving, Becoming: A New Focus for Education. Association for Supervision and Curriculum Development, 1962, Chapters 5 through 15,

Waetjen, Walter B., *Learning and Mental Health in the School.* Association for Supervision and Curriculum Development, 1966, Chapter 5, "Self-Actualization: A New Focus for Education," Chapter 6: "Learning and Becoming—New Meanings to Teachers," pp 99-146.

The Way Teaching Is: *Report of the Seminar on Teaching.* Association for Supervision and Curriculum Development and the Center for the Study of Instruction, 1966, pp 1-80.

School Management. May 1967, "Are You Afraid of Flexible Scheduling?" pp 97-108.

Members of the workshop were given copies of the following materials as part of the workshop program:

Differentiated Teaching Staff, Intern Seminar, March 15, 1967, Stanford University.

Allen, Dwight, W., *A Differentiated Teaching Staff,* Unpublished research paper, Stanford University.

Cooper, James M., *Developing Specific Teaching Skill Through Micro-Teaching,* Unpublished research paper, Stanford University.

Allen, Dwight W., *Micro-Teaching: A New Framework for In-Service Education,* Unpublished research paper, Stanford University.

Allen, Dwight W., and Young, David B., *Television Recordings, A New Dimension in Teacher Education.*

Shutes, R. E., *Research Reports,* Unpublished research reports, Palo Alto Senior High School, Palo Alto, California.

TOPICS OF THE REPORTS

Attention: Objectives; Classroom Climate-Dominative vs. Integrative Teaching Patterns; Classroom Climate-Anxiety and Achievement; Classroom Climate-Discipline; Classroom Climate-Compulsion, Anxiety, and the need for Structure; Classroom Climate-Warmth, Efficiency, and Dependence; Categories of Teaching Behavior; Range of Teaching Behavior; Group versus Individual Attention; Teaching for Retention; Motivation-Functions of Reinforcement; Motivation-Convergent vs. Divergent Thinking; Evaluation-Explicitness in Oral Responses; Evaluation-Effect of Comments on Motivation.

Offerings and Course Description 1966-67, Henry M. Gunn Senior High School, 780 Arastradero Road, Palo Alto, California.

Report of Independent Study Workshop, Sir Francis Drake High School, June 20—July 1, 1966, San Anselmo, California.

Educators Workshop, June 27, 1967, "How to Select Good Teachers," Pacific Telephone Co., Interviewer Training Center, 55 New Montgomery Street, Room 719, San Francisco, California. Mr. K. E. Hettick.

A copy of all of the above materials is available in the Redwood High School Faculty Library. Each member of the Curriculum Associates Workshop also has a complete set of the above materials.

APPENDIX "B"

SURVEY OF POLICIES RELATING TO EMPLOYMENT, RELEASED TIME, AND EXTRA PAY FOR DEPARTMENT HEADS IN PUBLIC, JUNIOR AND SENIOR HIGH SCHOOLS IN THE STATE OF CALIFORNIA[23]

DEPARTMENT CHAIRMEN

1. By Grade Span:

(e.g. Of the 10 schools in the Grades 6-8 group, none replied to question. Of the 72 schools in the Grades 7-8 group, 1 reported 4 positions; 3 reported 5 positions; 1 reported 6 positions, etc. 58 did not reply.)

Grades	Positions Assigned		No Reply
	Number Schools	Number Positions	
6-8			10
7-8	1	4	
	3	5	
	1	6	
	1	7	
	2	8	
	2	9	
	3	10	
	1	12	58
7-9	1	1	
	5	2	
	3	3	
	4	4	
	7	5	
	3	6	
	5	7	
	2	8	
	1	9	
	5	10	
	7	11	
	28	12	
	3	13	
	3	14	
	2	15	
	1	17	118

1.   (Continued)

| Grades | Positions Assigned | | No Reply |
	Number Schools	Number Positions	
8 - 9	1	11	
	1	13	1
7 - 12	1	2	
	2	3	
	1	6	
	1	7	
	1	8	
	1	12	17
9 - 11			9
9 - 12	7	1	
	5	2	
	2	3	
	4	4	
	8	5	
	4	6	
	3	7	
	10	8	
	11	9	
	11	10	
	6	11	
	44	12	
	18	13	
	10	14	148
10 - 12	2	1	
	2	2	
	2	3	
	4	5	
	1	6	
	1	7	
	7	8	
	5	9	
	5	10	
	5	11	

1. (Continued)

Grades	Position Assigned		No Reply
	Number Schools	Number Positions	
	15	12	
	8	13	
	5	14	
	3	15	
	1	16	48

1.1 *Subject Areas in Which Department Chairmen Are Given a Released Period for Department Chairman Duties.* (By grade span; see 2.1 for tabulation by ada.)

(e.g. Schools granting a released period to the Art Department Chairman: 10 in Grades 7-9; 2 in Grades 8-9; 2 in Grades 7-12; 42 in Grades 9-12; 23 in Grades 10-12.)

SUBJECT AREAS	GRADES							
	6-8	7-8	7-9	8-9	7-12	9-11	9-12	10-12
Art			10	2	2		42	23
Business			6	1	3	2	79	52
English		8	58	1	5	6	129	63
Foreign Language		4	22	1	4	2	77	24
Homemaking		2	10	2	3		46	24
Industrial Education		2	15		3	3	71	42
Mathematics		9	50		4	3	97	49
Music		1	9		3	1	34	16
Phys. Educ. - Boys		6	22		4	4	100	48
Phys. Educ. - Girls		2	11		3	1	60	37

1.1   (Continued)

SUBJECT AREAS	GRADES							
	6-8	7-8	7-9	8-9	7-12	9-11	9-12	10-12
Science		7	38		3	3	94	55
Social Science		8	52		3	3	109	57
Other			1			2	14	7

1.2   *Extra Pay for Department Chairmen.* (By Grade span; see 2.2 for tabulation by ada.)

	GRADES							
	6-8	7-8	7-9	8-9	7-12	9-11	9-12	10-12
Yes		7	73	2	7	7	165	73
No	4	30	93	1	12	1	98	36
No Reply	6	35	32		5	1	28	5

1.3   *Scale of Extra pay for Department Chairmen.* (By Grade span; see 2.3 for tabulation by ada.)

SCALE	GRADES							
	6-8	7-8	7-9	8-9	7-12	9-11	9-12	10-12
To $100		1					1	
$101 - $190			3				15	
$200 - $295			9	1	1		36	13
$300 - $395		2	4		2	4	31	5
$400 - $495			7	1			7	4
$500 - $590						1	2	1
$600 - $690							2	5
Over $700							1	

2.   By Average Daily Attendance:

	Positions Assigned		
ADA	Number Schools	Number Positions	No Reply

Grades 6 - 9

Under 500

	1	5	17

501 - 1200

	4	2	
	3	3	
	5	4	
	7	5	
	4	6	
	4	7	
	4	8	
	3	9	
	7	10	
	5	11	
	15	12	
	3	13	
	1	14	
	1	15	125

1201 - 2500

	1	2	
	2	5	
	2	7	
	1	10	
	3	11	
	11	12	
	1	13	
	2	14	
	1	15	
	1	17	44

Over 2500

	3	12	2

Grades 7 - 12

Under 500

	3	1	
	3	2	

2. (Continued)

| ADA | Positions Assigned | | No Reply |
	Number Schools	Number Positions	
	2	3	
	2	4	
	1	5	
	2	6	
	1	8	
	1	12	63
501 - 1200	4	1	
	1	2	
	1	3	
	2	4	
	3	5	
	3	6	
	8	8	
	5	9	
	3	10	
	3	11	
	7	12	
	6	13	
	3	14	53
1201 - 2500	2	1	
	3	2	
	3	3	
	6	5	
	2	6	
	3	7	
	7	8	
	11	9	
	14	10	
	7	11	
	46	12	
	17	13	
	8	14	
	2	15	84

2. (Continued)

Positions Assigned

ADA	Number Schools	Number Positions	No Reply
Over 2500	1	2	
	1	5	
	2	7	
	2	8	
	1	10	
	1	11	
	6	12	
	3	13	
	3	14	
	2	15	
	1	16	20

2.1 *Subject Areas in Which Department Chairmen are Given a Released Period for Department Chairman Duties.* (By average daily attendance; see 1.1 for tabulation by grade span.)

(e.g. Number of schools in the Grades 6-9 group granting a released period to the Art Department Chairman: under 500 ada, none; 501-1200 ada, 2; 1201-2500 ada, 3; over 2500 ada, 1.)

SUBJECT AREAS	a) GRADES 6-9 ADA				b) GRADES 7-12 ADA			
	Under 500	501-1200	1201-2500	Over 2500	Under 500	501-1200	1201-2500	Over 2500
Art		2	3	1	3	9	41	14
Business		1	1	1	5	25	82	24
English		16	28	4	12	44	120	27
Foreign Lang.		9	8	1	4	22	78	20
Homemaking		3	8	2	4	8	44	16

3. (Continued)

SUBJECT AREAS	a) GRADES 6-9 ADA				b) GRADES 7-12 ADA			
	Under 500	501-1200	1201-2500	Over 2500	Under 500	501-1200	1201-2500	Over 2500
Industrial Ed.		2	5	1	5	22	70	22
Mathematics	1	13	26	4	6	33	89	26
Music		3	3	1	2	8	32	11
Phys. Educ. - Boys		10	4	2	10	27	95	26
Phys. Educ. - Girls		3	3	2	3	13	65	22
Science		13	18	2	6	30	93	25
Social Science		14	27	4	5	36	105	27
Other			1		1	1	9	1

2.2   *Extra Pay for Department Chairmen.* (By average daily attendance; see 1.2 for tabulation by grade span.)

	a) GRADES 6-9 ADA				b) GRADES 7-12 ADA			
	Under 500	501-1200	1201-2500	Over 2500	Under 500	501-1200	1200-2500	Over 2500
Yes	1	45	33	3	10	52	153	38
No	9	94	23	2	39	42	61	5
No Reply	8	52	13		29	8	1	

2.3   *Scale of Extra Pay for Department Chairmen.* (By average daily attendance; see 1.3 for tabulation by grade span.)

2.3 (Continued)

SCALE	a) GRADES 6-9 ADA				b) GRADES 7-12 ADA			
	Under 500	501-1200	1201-2500	Over 2500	Under 500	501-1200	1201-2500	Over 2500
To $100							1	
$100 - $190		2	2			6	12	
$200 - $295		7	2		1	14	30	5
$300 - $395	1	5			4	11	24	3
$400 - $495		3	4			4	8	
$500 - $595							4	6
$600 - $695							1	
Over $700							1	

APPENDIX "C"

SELECTED EXAMPLES OF JOB DESCRIPTIONS ESTABLISHED FOR DEPARTMENT HEADS IN SCHOOL DISTRICTS IN THE UNITED STATES

SAN MATEO, CALIFORNIA*

A. Responsibility

A department head is a teacher who has been delegated by his principal, and approved by the Board of Trustees, to perform supervisory and administrative duties essential to the efficient operation of the department to which he has been assigned. The basic responsibility of the department head is to provide professional leadership within his department in the following areas:

    a. Supervision of personnel and curriculum
    b. Administration of departmental services and responsibilities

B. Supervision of Personnel and Curriculum

1. Recommends to the principal the scheduling of classes and the assignment of personnel in the department.
2. Assists the principal in the screening, selection, and orientation of personnel in the department.
3. Interprets to and advises departmental personnel on school and district policy.
4. Observes teachers in classrooms for the purpose of giving instructional aid and advice.
5. Assists the principal in evaluation procedures.
6. Coordinates departmental curriculum development and helps define the department's educational products and services.
7. Assists the teachers of the department with current developments (philosophy, practices, materials) within the areas of the department.
8. Confers with department members about student needs, teaching methods, materials, techniques, and subject matter.
9. Provides opportunities for the exchange of ideas regarding methods and resources within the department.
10. Coordinates textbook evaluation studies within the department.

---

*Reprinted by permission of the San Mateo Union High School District.

11. Consults with the superintendent and/or his staff concerning matters related to the department.

12. Cooperates with elementary schools and colleges toward the development of an articulated program.

13. Assists substitute teachers assigned to the department.

14. Assists in the placement of student observers and student teachers assigned to the department.

C. Administration of Departmental Services and Responsibilities

1. Acts as liaison between the school and district administration and the members of the department.

2. Represents the department in the formulation of school policy related to his subject area.

3. Plans and conducts department meetings.

4. Attends grade level and special subject meetings as required.

5. Participates in school department head meetings, district council meetings, and other special meetings as required.

6. Attends professional conferences and institutes and makes reports.

7. Informs student, faculty, and the community of the program of the department.

8. In cooperation with guidance department personnel, recommends the placement and assignment of students to subject sections in the department.

9. Assists the principal in the development and administration of the departmental budget.

10. Confers with sales representatives in and out of school regarding books, equipment, supplies, etc.

11. Requisitions textbooks and other instructional materials for the department.

12. Requisitions equipment and supplies for the department.

13. Confers with the district business department concerning specialized departmental needs.

14. Supervises equipment inventory and equipment repair within the department.

15. Completes all departmental reports and surveys.

16. Receives and distributes departmental correspondence.

17. Coordinates student participation in departmental-related contests, societies, and conferences.
18. Hosts visitors to the department.

ARCADIA, CALIFORNIA[24]

Under the general direction of the principal, the duties and responsibilities of department chairmen are as follows:

1. Call periodic meetings of his department to conduct necessary business.
2. Participate in called district-wide curriculum meetings to help plan proper articulation between segments of the instructional program in specific subject areas.
3. Assist in the selection of textbooks and other instructional materials for his department.
4. Order instructional supplies and equipment for his department; submit requisitions to the assistant principal.
5. Keep the principal informed of the activities of the department and contemplated recommendations regarding the instructional program.
6. Organize the department for the improvement of teaching.
7. Prepare the preliminary budget.
8. Develop the program of studies.
9. Be responsible for the selection, distribution, inventory rotation, and storage of all departmental supplies.
10. Work with the principal on all matters pertaining to the program of the department.
11. Work for unity and harmony and a high *esprit de corps* within the department and with the total staff.
12. Be thoroughly familiar with the educational philosophy, objectives, methods, and courses of study of the district which apply to the department and provide creative leadership in their understanding, acceptance, and utilization.
13. Interpret rules, regulations, policies, and procedures to members of the department, reviewing with the principal beforehand all problems involving clarity and/or differences of opinion.

14. Maintain and promote professional growth of the members.

15. Hold special department meetings as the need arises.

16. Review all annual budgetary needs.

17. Give advice or assistance to members of the department whenever requested or deemed advisable for the maintenance or development of sound educational practices.

18. Through the librarian, keep all members of the department continuously familiar with available text book and resource materials, and recommend additional needs to the library.

19. Assist the principal in the development of all effective public relations programs in order that the public may at all times be kept intelligently and adequately informed about the work of the school. *(Suggestion:* Prepare news releases on interesting and unusual happenings in the department such as: individual class or student achievement; individual classroom or departmental activities; any unusual achievement of a teacher.)

20. Assist the principal in correlating the work of the several departments to the end that the program of the school be a unified whole.

21. Plan and hold department meetings to discuss problems pertaining to the improvement of instruction as well as general department problems.

22. Give minutes of department meetings to the principal.

23. Make available to all teachers in the department teaching materials and aids which have been developed by individual teachers.

24. Perform other duties as assigned by the principal.

* * * *

SACRAMENTO, CALIFORNIA[24]

In order to become eligible as a candidate for a position as senior high school department chairman on a permanent basis, an applicant should possess the following minimum qualifications:

1. A clear general secondary credential or other clear credential issued under revised state certification regulations which authorizes services in the subject field to be supervised.

2.   A major in the subject field to be supervised. (If the
      bachelor's degree is in education, the master's degree must
      be in the subject field.)

3.   A master's degree.

4.   The recommendation of the applicant's principal.

5.   The recommendation of the assistant superintendent,
      secondary schools.

6.   A minimum of three years of successful teaching in the
      field to be supervised at the senior high school level.

BROCKTON, MASSACHUSETTS[24]

1. The heads of departments shall, under the immediate direc-
    tion of the head master, supervise the work of the teachers
    in their departments, visit the classes as often as possible
    during the year, and render to the head master not later
    than the first week of march a report of their observations
    relative to the work and qualifications of each teacher. The
    report shall be considered in questions of re-election.

2. They shall outline the work of their departments in accord-
    ance with the course of study laid down by the school
    board and shall consult with the head master about all
    changes in the course of study affecting their departments.
    When the work of a department in the high school is a
    continuation of work done in the grades, the head of the
    department may be consulted regarding any changes in the
    course of study in the grades.

3. Heads of departments shall teach regularly in the depart-
    ment.

4. They shall have general supervision of all activities
    connected with, or assigned to, their departments.

5. They shall make a quarterly report of the work and
    financial transactions of their departments to the head
    master.

6. They shall meet with the teachers of the department
    quarterly for discussion of the work of the department.

7. The head master shall call a meeting of the heads of
    departments at least four times during the school year.

8. Heads of departments shall have charge of the books and of the supplies issued to departments and shall make an inventory and report of same to the head master at the close of the school year. They shall make requisitions for supplies and recommendations for the adoption and purchase of books to the head master.

9. They shall make a report to the head master of the condition and progress of their departments at the end of the school year, together with such suggestions for changes and improvements as, in their opinions, would make their departments more efficient. They shall draw up schedules of work for teachers in their departments.

10. They shall perform such other duties as the head master or school board shall direct.

11. A master's degree or its equivalent shall be required of all candidates for the position of head of a department.

* * *

DETROIT, MICHIGAN[24]

Specific Requirements

I. Experience

    A. Three years of successful contract teaching experience in senior high, junior high, or technical schools.

II. Education

    A. Master's degree or doctor's degree from an institution accredited by the North Central Association of Colleges and Secondary Schools or equivalent agency.

    B. Valid Michigan teaching certificate covering grades 7-12 inclusive.

    C. Twenty-four semester hours of preparation in the subject field elected as a department head. (If the North Central Association raises its requirements prior to the time of appointment as a department head, the candidate must meet these requirements before an appointment to department head can be effected.)

Duties and Responsibilities

In secondary schools (senior high, junior high, and technical) the staff includes department heads who work under the direction of the principal. In general, department heads serve in these capacities:

I.   Represent the department at meetings of department heads or wherever department needs representation.

II. Chair meetings of teachers of department.

III. Assume leadership in seeing that the program of the entire department is advanced and maintained to the highest possible and balanced level, and coordinated with other departments.

IV. See that staff members in the department, especially new personnel, receive such assistance and information as will help them to do the best possible job.

V.   Carry on such other responsibilities for the department as assigned by the principal.

The department head's responsibilities are very important, and the demands upon his abilities and resourcefulness great. Candidates for department heads should be persons of mature judgment, cheerful disposition, great tact, and physical stamina. They should have successful teaching experience, acquaintance with community agencies, and a knowledge of curriculum and instructional materials. The personality of the department head is of importance, for the way he appears to and works with others will have a great deal to do with his ability to win and keep the confidence of his students, his teachers, and his colleagues.

* * * *

ARDSLEY, NEW YORK[24]

Duties of Department Head

A.   He shall regularly demonstrate initiative and leadership in the improvement of the instructional program of his department.

B.   He shall take an active and energetic role in curriculum improvement in his department throughout the year.

C.   He shall develop a continuous program of curriculum evaluation.

D.   He shall analyze standard test results as related to curriculum content.

E.   He shall analyze college board scores and college freshman marks in terms of our curriculum, instructional program, marking system, and standards of achievement.

F.   He shall carry out the following personnel and administrative functions:

1.   Personnel
(a) Supervise classroom instruction.
(b) Make recommendations regarding evaluations.

2.   Finance
(a) Collect and prepare all information pertaining to the preparation of budgetary requirements on a three-year basis.
(b) Inventory and be responsible for books, equipment, and supplies allocated to his department.
(c) Appraise and act on requisitions for his department as may be required.

G.   Department heads may be called upon from time to time for written reports or evaluations as conditions may require.

Size of Department

Secondary department heads may be appointed in special subject matter, where six or more teachers are employed on a year-to-year assignment. In subject matter fields of less than six teachers, a temporary chairman may be appointed by the high school principal from year to year, with no additional compensation, if such is required in order to facilitate certain administrative and coordinating responsibilities.

Appointment of Department Heads

Secondary department heads or acting department heads are to be recommended to the board of education by the supervising principal after consultation with the high school principal based upon educational training and qualities of leadership, intellectual interest, instructional "know-how," interest in and desire for curriculum improvement and coordination within his department, and throughout the school and the system in his field of specialization.

Responsibility and Time

A department head may be given no more than three periods per day (of a seven-period day, or one less than the regular teaching load)—depending upon the size of the department, for the purpose of administering, supervising, and evaluating the work of his department. In addition to the foregoing, he is responsible for coordinating and preparing curricular materials, as well as keeping current on curricular developments.

Length of Appointment

Secondary department heads shall be appointed for a period of one year, and appointments are to be made on or before July 1st if recommended by the supervising principal.

* * * * * *

GREAT NECK, NEW YORK[24]

Upon recommendation of the superintendent, the board may from time to time appoint members of the staff to act as heads of instructional departments in the junior and senior high schools. A department head shall:

1. Assist in outlining and revising the work of his department consistent with courses of study recommended by the state education department.

2. Hold meetings and conferences with teachers in his department regarding courses of study, methods of instruction, and matters affecting the progress of pupils; and, in general, render assistance to staff members, especially those new to the department.

3. Recommend the assignment of classes and work schedules of the teachers in his department; and report, at a time designated by the principal, his observations relative to the work and qualifications of each probationary teacher and of such other teachers as may be determined by the principal.

4. Plan with teachers of the department attendance at appropriate conferences in the light of values to the department,

money appropriated for conference attendance, and fair representation.

5. Submit to the principal, at the end of the school year, a written report of the work and progress of his department, together with suggestions for changes and improvements.

6. Prepare and submit to the principal, budget estimates for the ensuing year.

7. Make recommendations for the adoption of textbooks and for the purchase of equipment and supplies for the department.

8. See that departmental books, equipment, and supplies are properly cared for and inventoried, and that all money due for lost books and equipment is collected and remitted to the principal each month.

9. Perform such other supervisory duties as may be assigned to him or the department by the superintendent or the principal.

ADMINISTRATIVE PROCEDURES AND JOB DESCRIPTION ESTABLISHED IN A DISTRICT IN WHICH DEPARTMENT HEADS ARE ELECTED RATHER THAN APPOINTED*

Jefferson Union High School District, Daly City, California

DEPARTMENT HEADS AND CHAIRMEN

Provisions of this section become effective with the next department election conducted.

ESTABLISHMENT OF

The position of Department Head or Chairman shall be created when the requisite number of hours are taught within a subject area. Several subject areas grouped together is not justification for a department except that a Fine Arts Department shall be established by grouping together Art, Music, Drama and Photography providing that the teaching hours requirement is met.

---

*Reprinted by permission of the Jefferson Union High School District.

METHOD OF SELECTION

Necessary elections shall be conducted by the principal in January each year, election will be by secret ballot. At least two persons shall be nominated at each election. Each teacher shall have one vote in the election of the Department Head and/or Chairman for each class that he teaches in the department. (A Department Head's supervision period shall be looked upon as a teaching period.)

DEFINITIONS

Head

A Department Head is the person elected or appointed to coordinate and supervise the activities of a subject area department in which at least twenty-five hours are taught. One of the twenty-five hours may be the department head period.

Chairmen

A Department Chairman is the person elected or appointed to coordinate and supervise the activities of a subject area department in which at least fifteen hours are taught.

Because of a unique control situation in Physical Education, in addition to a Department Head a Department Chairman of the opposite sex shall be selected in the prescribed manner.

TERM OF OFFICE

Department Heads and Chairmen shall be elected by faculty members of a department for a term of three years pursuant with the election procedure established and approved by the Administrative Council. (See *New Schools* exception below.)

When a Department Head or Chairman is, in the judgement of the principal, performing unsatisfactory service, goes on Sabbatical Leave, or is otherwise unable to serve, the principal shall appoint another Department Head or Chairman for the remainder of the school year. In addition, a Department Head or Chairman may be removed for failure to carry out the responsibilities of his position before his term expires if a majority of the members of said department request the principal to hold a "removal election," and if at said election a majoirty of the department cast ballots in favor of the removal. If the Department Head or Chairman is removed from office by this method, the principal shall appoing an Acting Department Head or Chairman for the remainder of the school year.

If a Department Head or Chairman is removed from office by either of the above procedures, the principal shall prior to the close of said year, pursuant with the district's election rules and regulations hold an election to select a Department Head or Chairman for a new three-year term.

NEW SCHOOLS

New schools shall receive special consideration in establishment of departments and may, provided sufficient growth is projected for the following year, establish a department one year early.

In the case of a new school, Department Heads and/or Chairmen shall be appointed by the principal for a period of one full school year, after which they will be elected in the manner prescribed above.

QUALIFICATIONS AND COMPENSATIONS

1. A Department Head or Chairman:

    a. Must have tenure. This may be waived by the Administrative Council.

    b. Must have completed 30 units after the AB degree and/or hold a Master's degree, in the subject field he leads. Total fulfillment of this requirement may be waived by the Administrative Council, providing the individual nominated and/or elected for said position has embarked upon an educational program leading to the fulfillment of this requirement.

2. Compensation:

    a. A Department Head shall be compensated at a yearly rate established by the Board of Trustees and shall receive an additional supervisory period other than the normal preparation period for carrying out departmental duties.

    b. A Department Chairman shall be compensated at a yearly rate established by the Board of Trustees but shall not receive an additional supervisory period other than his normal preparation period.

A.   General Responsibilities:

He shall, under the direction of the Principal, coordinate the activities of the department.

He shall perform such specific duties as may be adopted by the Board of Trustees or assigned by the District or School Administration. Specific duties include but are not limited to the following:

B.   Specific Duties:

Instruction

He shall work with the Assistant Principal-Instruction toward improvement of curriculum and instruction.

He shall develop and evaluate objectives and courses of study within the department and relate such courses and objectives to the offerings of other departments.

He shall periodically review and evaluate the course of study and if necessary recommend curriculum revision.

He shall coordinate units of his department with the District Instruction Director.

He shall provide in-service training and report to his department on observations, conferences, local courses and standards and promising practices in the field.

He shall establish in cooperation with the Guidance Department a program of suitable diagnostic tests and related procedures for such purposes as placement, promotion, standards of achievement and evaluation.

He shall review textbooks and other supplementary materials and make necessary recommendations to the principal and the Instruction Department.

Administration

He shall act in a liaison capacity between his teachers and the Administration.

He shall advise in the selection, evaluation, retention and/or dismissal of teachers within the department.

He shall meet with his teachers monthly.

He shall assist in making a tentative schedule of classes for his department.

He shall assist the Administration in planning subject and class-room assignments within his department.

He shall prepare the departmental budget.

He shall be responsible for the inventory, care and use of departmental supplies and equipment.

He shall administer the department use of facilities and equipment, such as library and Audio-Visual aids.

He shall attend meetings related to his duties which are called by the principal, instruction Department or Superintendent.

He shall prepare a yearly report sending the original to each principal and a copy to the Superintendent, stating the progress made in the curriculum and instruction in the department, plans for future improvements, and the problems needing solution.

REFERENCE CITATIONS

-1- David Bork, "DSC (Departmental Specialist —Leader for Quality Instruction," Minnesota *Journal of Education,* 47, March 1967, p. 19

-2- Melvin G. Hipps, "Supervision: A Basic Responsibility of the Department Head," *Clearing House,* 39, April 1965, pp. 488-489

-3- Leon M. Lessinger, "Essays on the Superintendency, Part IV," (unpublished paper, San Mateo, Calif.), p. 1

-4- James R. Squire, Roger K. Applebee, and Robert J. Lacampagne, *High School Departments of English: Their Organization, Administration, and Supervision,* (Champaign, Ill.: National Council of Teachers of English, 1965), p. 13

-5- Michael G. Callahan, "Recommendations for the Improvement of Department Head Policies and Practices in the San Mateo Union High School District," (unpublished paper, San Mateo, Calif.), pp. 3-4

-6- Kenneth Easterday, "The Department Chairman—What Are his Duties and Qualifications?" *Bulletin of the National Association of Secondary School Principals,* 49, October 1965, p. 81

-7- Stanley L. Clement, "Choosing the Department Head," *Bulletin of the National Association of Secondary School Principals,* 45, October 1961, pp. 48-52
Ned W. Bowler, "Who Should Be in Charge of the Department—Head or Chairman?" *Journal of Higher Education,* 33, June 1962, pp. 315-318

-8- *Bulletin of the National Association of Secondary School Principals,* 49, p. 80

-9- Donald C. Manlove and Robert Buser, "The Department Head: Myths and Reality," *Bulletin of the National Association of Secondary School Principals,* 50, October 1965, p. 106

-10- Squire, Applebee, and Lacampagne, *High School Departments of English,* p. 25

-11- Squire, Applebee, and Lacampagne, *High School Departments of English* p. 15

-12- National Education Association, American Association of School Administrators and Research Division, *Department*

Heads in Senior High Schools, Educational Research Reporter, January 1966, pp. 2-6

-13- *Bulletin of the National Association of Secondary School Principals,* 50, p. 106

-14- Clarence Fielstra, "Instructional Improvement Behaviors of Secondary School Department Chairmen," *California Journal for Instructional Improvement,* 10, October 1967, pp. 216-224

-15- *California Journal for Instructional Improvement,* 10, pp. 222-23

-16- Charles Wallace, "An Administrative Organization Designed for Instructional Improvement," *Bulletin of the National Association of Secondary School Principals,* 45, February 1961, pp. 32-35

-17- R. Baird Shuman, "Departmental Chairmen or Heads of Divisions?" *Clearing House,* 40, March 1966, pp. 429-431

-18- *Clearing House,* 39, pp. 487-491

-19- Donald Thomas, "Which Organization—Department or Division—for Your School?" *Bulletin of the National Association of Secondary School Principals,* 49, October 1965, pp. 49-58

-20- *Bulletin of the National Association of Secondary School Principals,* 49, p. 53

-21- *Bulletin of the National Association of Secondary School Principals,* 50, pp. 99-107

-22- *Bulletin of the National Association of Secondary School Principals,* 50, p. 104

-23- Myron Greene, Norman Shapiro, and Alexander W. Winchester, *Survey of Secondary School Administrative Organization,* (Burlingame, Calif.: California Association of Secondary School Administrators, 1967), pp. 27-34

-24- *Department Heads in Senior High Schools,* pp. 7-13

BIBLIOGRAPHY

Bork, David, "DSC (Departmental Specialist Chairman)—Leader for Quality Instruction," Minnesota *Journal of Higher Education*, 47, p. 19, (March, 1967)

Browning, E. R., "The Ideal Department Chairman," *National Business Education Quarterly*, 30, pp. 42-47, (May, 1962)

Bowler, Ned W., "Who Should Be in Charge of the Department—Head or Chairman?" *Journal of Higher Education*, 33, pp. 315-318, (June, 1962)

Callahan, Michael G., "Recommendations for the Improvement of Department Head Policies and Practices in the San Mateo Union High School District," (unpublished paper, San Mateo, Calif.)

Clement, Stanley L., "Choosing the Department Head," *Bulletin of the National Association of Secondary School Principals*, 45, pp. 48-52, (October, 1961)

Easterday, Kenneth, "The Department Chairman—What Are His Duties and Qualifications?" *Bulletin of the National Association of Secondary School Principals*, 49, pp. 77-85, (October, 1965)

Fielstra, Clarence, "Instructional Improvement Behaviors of Secondary School Department Chairmen," *California Journal for Instructional Improvement*, 10, pp. 216-224, (October, 1967)

Greene, Myron; Shapiro, Norman; and Winchester, Alexander W., *Survey of Secondary School Administrative Organization*. Burlingame, Calif.: California Association of Secondary School Administrators, 1967

Grieder, Calvin, "Let High School Department Heads Be Responsible for Supervision of Instruction," *Nation's Schools*, 71, pp. 8+, (April, 1963)

High, Paul B., "The Supervisory Role of the Department Head," *Clearing House*, 40, pp. 213-215, (December, 1965)

Hipps, G. Melvin, "Supervision: A Basic Responsibility of the Department Head," *Clearing House*, 39, pp. 487-491, (April, 1965)

Kidd, Jim L., "The Department Headship and the Supervisory Role," *Bulletin of the National Association of Secondary School Principals*, 49, pp. 70-76, (October, 1965)

Lessinger, Leon M., "Essays on the Superintendency, Part IV," (unpublished paper, San Mateo, Calif.)

Maczuga, P., "Selecting Department Heads," *Clearing House*, 37, pp. 239-241, (December, 1962)

Manlove, Donald C., and Buser, Robert, "The Department Head: Myths and Reality," *Bulletin of the National Association of Secondary School Principals*, 50, pp. 99-107, (November, 1966)

247

Martin, T.B., "The Business Education Department Head in the Changing Secondary School," *Balance Sheet,* 47, pp. 12-16+, (September, 1965)

National Education Association, American Association of School Administrators and Research Division. *Department Heads in Senior High Schools.* Educational Research Service Reporter. Washington, D.C.: the Association, January, 1966. 13 p., 10 cents

"Report of Curriculum Associates Workshop," (unpublished paper, Larkspur, Calif.)

Satlow, I.D., "Profile of the Successful Department Head," *Business Education World,* 43, pp. 14-16, (April, 1963)

Shuman, R. Baird, "Departmental Chairmen or Heads of Divisions?" *Clearing House,* 40, pp. 429-431, (March, 1966)

Squire, James R.; Applebee, Roger K.; and Lacampagne, Robert J., *High School Departments of English: Their Organization, Administration, and Supervision.* Champaign, Ill.: National Council of Teachers of English, 1965

Stephenson, Claude E., "Departmental Organization for Better Instruction," *Bulletin of the National Association of Secondary School Principals,* 45, pp. 9-14, (December, 1961)

Thomas, Donald, "Which Organization—Department or Division—for Your School?" *Bulletin of the National Association of Secondary School Principals,* 49, pp. 49-57, (October, 1965)

Wallace, Charles, "An Administrative Organization Designed for Instructional Improvement," *Bulletin of the National Association of Secondary School Principals,* 45, pp. 32-35, (February, 1961)

Waltham, W. A., "A High School Department Head Views Supervision," *National Business Education Quarterly,* 29, pp. 24-27+, (May, 1961)

Veidemanis, G., "Frankly Speaking: A Candid View of the Department Chairman's Role," *English Journal,* 56, pp. 828-833, (September, 1967)

Index